The Sixties

PASSION, POLITICS, AND STYLE

Edited by Dimitry Anastakis

McGill-Queen's University Press

Montreal & Kingston | London | Ithaca

© McGill-Queen's University Press 2008
ISBN 978-0-7735-3321-9 (cloth)
ISBN 978-0-7735-3322-6 (paper)

Legal deposit second quarter 2008
Bibliothèque nationale du Québec

Printed in Canada on acid-free paper that is 100% ancient forest free
(100% post-consumer recycled), processed chlorine free

This book has been published with the help of a grant from the Canadian
Federation for the Humanities and Social Sciences, through the Aid to Scholarly
Publications Programme, using funds provided by the Social Sciences and
Humanities Research Council of Canada.

McGill-Queen's University Press acknowledges the support of the Canada
Council for the Arts for our publishing program. We also acknowledge the
financial support of the Government of Canada through the Book Publishing
Industry Development Program (BPIDP) for our publishing activities.

LIBRARY AND ARCHIVES CANADA CATALOGUING IN PUBLICATION

The sixties : passion, politics and style / edited by Dimitry Anastakis.
Includes bibliographical references and index.
ISBN 978-0-7735-3321-9 (bound)
ISBN 978-0-7735-3322-6 (pbk.)
1. Canada – Social conditions – 1945–1971. 2. Canada – History – 1963–.
3. Canada – History – 1945–1963. 4. Canada – Politics and government –
1963–1968. 5. Canada – Politics and government – 1957–1963. 6. Canada –
Politics and government – 1968–1979. 7. Canada – Intellectual life – 20th
century. 8. Nineteen sixties. I. Anastakis, Dimitry, 1970–
FC620.S59 2008   971.064'3   C2007-905753-5

Set in 10.5/14 Electra with Helvetica Neue
Book design & typesetting by Garet Markvoort, zijn digital

Contents

Illustrations

Acknowledgments

Many people deserve thanks for contributing to this collection in one way or another. First and foremost, a heartfelt thank-you goes to all the contributors for their efforts and patience. To the organizers of the conference that inspired this collection, Victoria Dickinson and Melanie Martens at the McCord Museum and Magda Fahrni in the Department of History at the Université du Québec à Montréal, thank you for bringing these authors together initially. At McGill-Queen's University Press, I would like to thank Philip Cercone, Joan McGilvray, Anushka Jonian, and Brenda Prince. Two anonymous assessors provided excellent comments and suggestions for revision. Bryan Palmer, my colleague at Trent University, was kind enough to read an earlier version of the introduction and provided very helpful comments. Finally, I would like to acknowledge the Aid to Scholarly Publications Programme, which provided financial assistance for this project.

The Sixties

1

Introduction

DIMITRY ANASTAKIS

For those who did not live through the experience of the Sixties, it is often difficult to comprehend this tumultuous period. Even those who lived through the era and have studied the Sixties have wrestled with its deeper meaning.[1] While the Sixties' ultimate "meaning" remains elusive, there can be no doubt that the period's transformative effect upon Canadians – culturally, politically, and economically – was immense. From arts and architecture to politics and protest, the decade has attained near-mythical status, leaving an undeniable influence on virtually every aspect of Canadian life. The images, sounds, and tastes of the decade remain an indelible part of our own twenty-first-century experience, a large part of our collective DNA, and a foundation for understanding our society as individuals, as Canadians, as North Americans, and as citizens of a larger world. Yet for a decade that remains so well defined within the public memory, the Sixties left behind an ambiguous historic legacy for those who study the period.[2]

The decade itself resists easy periodization. When did "the Sixties" really begin? The year 1960 marks the calendar beginning of the decade, but the era's explosion into consciousness as something new, something different, something dramatic is more often remembered symbolically. Perhaps it was the election of a romantic Camelotesque president south of the border; or the seeming end of innocence symbolized by that president's murder; or the screaming arrival of the Beatles. An era of so many memories, its beginnings are difficult to constrict to any single date or event. Similarly, there is no obvious terminus to the decade. The powerful generational influence of the baby boomers – who came of age in the Sixties and whose demographic, cultural, and political influence is still shaped in so many ways by this experience – begs the question of whether this remains the "endless decade," a nostalgic, never-ending summer of '67. After all, the many totems of the period – the music, the protests, the clothes, the *style* – remain seared into the collective memories of the generations that have come after the baby boomers. There remains a fist-shaking refusal to let go of the era in many aspects of our life. At the same time, the passion and irreverence of the decade ended imperceptibly and quietly, and lamentably seems to have been lost forever. So much happened between the screaming that accompanied the Beatles to the quiet surrender of the Weathermen that it feels more reasonable to think of the period as a series of memory mileposts, instead of some unbelievably short span of years.[3]

Periodization is further complicated by place and perspective. In the scattered, spacious, and sometimes Spartan country that was Canada, the inhabitants were at once intimately involved yet often peripheral to events that shaped the period. Canadians understood and took part in the great movements that wracked the generation, but they also had their own mental markers to demarcate the decade. While the Beatles' rollicking emergence might loom large, some might remember the triumphant yet difficult creation of a new flag in 1965 or might bask in the international glory of Expo '67 in Montreal or quicken with memories of 1968's Trudeaumania.[4] In Quebec, the 1960 election of Jean Lesage's Liberals marked newfound confidence, economic security, and a dramatic break from a conservative, parochial past. For Québécois, the Sixties were a bridge from the time of Maurice Duplessis and the *Grande noirceur* to a vibrant, progressive, and modern Quebec. Getting across that bridge may have been difficult, but we would not recognize the province or the country today if that journey had not been taken.[5]

The Quiet Revolution was pivotal to all Canadians' Sixties experience, for it helped shape the political and constitutional landscape for decades to come. Yet English-speaking Canadians' experience was also shaped by an undeniable American influence. Consumerism, culture, and conflict was a cross-border experience, and Canadians understood the Sixties as Americans, while at the same time often feeling just as vehemently anti-American. For English-speaking Canadians, the "otherness" of the United States was both a wellspring for their own cultural touchstones and a source of their determination to be different.[6] The same year that people in English Canada gloried in the freedom of the distinctively American "summer of love" and pounded their chests with American-like pride at the exploits of Expo '67, they sadly looked across the river to a Detroit aflame with the fury of racial conflict and urban destruction. The ambiguous legacy grew.

There were revolutions of another kind for so many Canadians during that period. Women and the gay community fought for sexual and legal rights that challenged the notions of gender and tradition. Students, artists, and intellectuals broke the shackles of past practice to challenge every shibboleth they could, often aping imported trends and ideas, but also shaping these concepts into distinctively Canadian approaches. Aboriginal Canadians loudly proclaimed a new approach to their dealings with white society, while immigrants and visible minorities asserted themselves forcefully as vibrant actors in an increasingly multiracial country. All these dramatic changes remain part of our understanding of the past and of our present experience, and all of them are central to the heated debate over the impact of the decade.[7]

Many of these issues are now coming into clearer focus. Canadian historians have begun to examine the Sixties from distinctive points of view, which build upon and at the same time often stand apart from currents found in the voluminous American interpretations of the era.[8] Yet while Canadian general histories of the postwar period have examined the well-tread political, economic, and social issues of the Sixties, they have also exhibited an overly dispassionate, clinical accounting of a period that was at turns passionate, profound, and profane.[9] Other works vividly recapture the passion of the era yet sometimes lack the objective (and often dispassionate) touch of a historian.[10] Important works from the period itself focus on traditional questions of politics and "nation," yet they seem to come from a different world, let alone the same decade: when set beside the riotous colours and raunchy rhetoric of the era, it is almost unbelievable that cranky conservative John Diefenbaker was the hero of the day for so many Canadians, or that George Grant's *Lament for a Nation* could be a defining tome. But Diefenbaker was a hero of the Sixties, and George Grant was a leading intellectual light.[11]

Newer scholarship has attempted to bridge the divide between the passionate testimonials of the Sixties' keenest chroniclers and the clinical appraisals posited in more traditional assessments of the era. Douglas Owram's "biography of the first twenty-five years of a generation," *Born at the Right Time: A History of the Baby Boom Generation*, is a general history of the period that focuses on the size, affluence, and power of the boomers who came to define the Sixties generation in Canada. Owram's work is an important step forward in the Canadian historiography in that it attempts to develop a broad treatment of the period, though the Sixties is the driving meme of the book. Other postwar examinations, such as Alvin Finkel's *Our Lives: Canada after 1945* and Magda Fahrni and Robert Rutherdale's *Creating Postwar Canada: Community, Diversity, and Dissent, 1945–1975*, also tackle the period, though few Canadian historians have attempted to synthesize the era itself. These works have all contributed to a small but growing literature that explores Canada since the Second World War, including the Sixties.[12]

At the same time, other works have focused more specifically on Canadian issues that fall under the rubric of larger North American themes that are elementary to "the Sixties." In understanding the period as one marked by protest and student uprisings, Canadian students once might have learned only of the Student Nonviolent Coordinating Committee (SNCC), or Students for a Democratic Society (SDS), or the riotous 1968 Democratic Convention in Chicago. Certainly, as Cyril Levitt has argued in *Children of Privilege: Student Revolt in the Sixties*, Canadian student revolt was part of a broader Western movement which Canadians turned on, tuned into, and fed off of.[13] Yet recent Canadian scholarship reminds us of the sometimes distinctive goals of the vibrant student movements in our own country in places as diverse as well-known Rochdale College in hippie Yorkville and protests in not so sleepy Saskatchewan.[14] Student groups such as the Combined Universities Campaign for Nuclear Disarmament (CUCND) or the Student Union for Peace Action (SUPA) are important elements of the Canadian story and deserve far more attention from Canadian scholars.[15]

Some good work has been done on the intellectual fount that helped propel these student movements forward. The New Left had its Canadian variations, some of which took a distinctively nationalist and (sometimes) anti-American tack. Scholarship that explores the emergence of the Waffle, the New Democratic Party's ultranationalist and socialist fragment, places the particularities of the Canadian New Left's demands within the broader spectrum of critiques of both the capitalist system and Canada's relations with the United States.[16] At the same time, work on the more "mainstream" economic nationalism that emerged in the Sixties helps explain why this variation of "new nationalism" became so popular among Canadians.[17] Canadian scholars are slowly coming to understand the connection between patrician Walter Gordon and the popular, popish, anti-Americanism exhibited in the Guess Who's obviously subversive "American Woman." Both sentiments sprang from the same source – the search for a distinctive Canadian voice at a time of tremendous change and conflict.

Of course, no discussion of the Sixties can be complete without addressing the twin issues of civil rights and Vietnam. In Canada, the main focus of the civil rights movement was on francophones in Quebec, who were transformed from *Canadiens français* to *Québécois* during the Quiet Revolution. Timely new work has explored and reconsidered the Quiet Revolution and has even gone so far as to question the "Quebec model" that emerged as a consensus from the period.[18] But Canadians should also remember that other groups experienced their own quiet revolutions. Acadians in New Brunswick succeeded in asserting themselves politically, just as Québécois had, and began to play a role on the provincial and national stages. Allophones, those Canadians of non-French and non-British descent, also asserted themselves in the Sixties and sparked their own multicultural revolution – sometimes in direct conflict with the biculturalism being championed by many anglophones and francophones at the very same time. Civil rights in Canada in the Sixties was as much about sound as it was about colour.[19] Where civil rights led, Vietnam followed. Although Canadians did not take part militarily, they were certainly on the domestic front lines in the battle over U.S. policy in Southeast Asia. War protests and condemnation of Canada's military industrial complex illustrated the unrelenting closeness, conflict, and contradictions of the country's relations with the United States. Canadian historians' focus on the Vietnam War has shifted, from dwelling on diplomatic manoeuvres and the question of Canada's "complicity," to examining the issue from different perspectives and using different optics. This is not surprising, given the country's unique contribution to the Vietnam discourse through the issue of war resisters, which historians such as John Hagan, Frank Kusch, and David Churchill have recently begun to explore from a more scholarly viewpoint.[20] Like so many aspects of Canadian history, scholarship on Vietnam provides familiar entry points yet leads in different directions when pushed beyond traditional parameters.

This collection aims both to add to all these debates and to generate new discussions by exploring a few of the strains of the period that make it so fascinating and contradictory. The commonalities of this disparate grouping are, of course, the Sixties, but they are much more than that. There is a sense of connectedness to the essays that causes them to defy categorization: gender, art, space, modernism, technology, culture, and protest all appear in some shape or form. They are thus divided, imprecisely, into three broad and sometimes intersecting themes: passion, politics, and style. Together, they present a multifaceted album of that pivotal decade and remind those who experienced the period, and those who did not, why the Sixties engender such passion even today. The essays vary widely in tone and style, a fact that reflects the diverse disciplines represented here, as well as the eclectic styles of the period. Touching upon such a wide range of subjects and utilizing various styles and visual materials to impart some sense of the decade, they also typify the diversity and excitement of emerging scholarship, focused as they are on an era that, in Canada at least, is only now hitting its stride as an area of serious study.

The aforementioned themes of passion, politics and style come together particularly well in the reminiscences of the collection's first contributor, Quebec journalist Gretta Chambers. As one of the few anglophone females reporting on the province in the Sixties, Chambers had a front-row view of the Quiet Revolution and the tumultuous changes it ushered in. Her penetrating analysis of those heady, hectic, and often heated times sets the tone for the collection and allows the reader to gain a sense of the Sixties. While Chambers's focus is on the passion and politics of the period in Quebec, she also leaves no doubt that "the style adopted as the decade dawned was one of daring."

Above all, the Sixties were defined by their passion. The counterculture, Vietnam, civil rights, and so many other movements and events were sparked by a passion for challenging preconceived notions and traditional approaches to politics, art, and protest. Indeed, protest remains a singular trope of the Sixties. From the 1963 March on Washington to the conflagrations of Quebec students supporting the extremist Front de libération du Québec (FLQ) during the October Crisis of 1970, protest was a constant of the period. Perhaps no other issue generated as much protest as America's involvement in Vietnam. Frances Early examines one chapter of that protest in her article on the Voice of Women of Canada (VOW) and its opposition to the Vietnam War. Early shows how VOW used distinctive approaches consistent with women's reform tradition, which at the same time prefigured the new feminist impulse of the late Sixties and developed a cogent female-centred critique of the war and the Canadian government's involvement in the U.S. war machine. These efforts included approaches as diverse as providing front-line female eyewitness accounts of the destruction from North Vietnam, humanitarian knitting projects that attracted widespread interest in the United States, and arranging exchanges for Vietnamese and American women, which aimed to open the channels of communication between women affected by the conflict as a way of underscoring female anti-war expression across the two nationalities. The group's gendered and maternalist approach to protest provoked wide response and was ultimately instrumental in advancing VOW's message of peace and understanding, a sentiment that remains a lasting legacy of VOW and the decade.

Passion plays a role, too, in Kristy Holmes's "Negotiating Citizenship: Joyce Wieland's *Reason over Passion*." In this article, the protest of the Sixties is channelled by Margaret Trudeau – the flower-child bride of outwardly hip Prime Minister Pierre Trudeau (elected 1968) – into a passionate attack on Trudeau's inwardly emotionless dictum of "Reason over passion." The symbolic yet physical target of Margaret's passion – Joyce Wieland's quilt artwork – becomes a canvas not only for Holmes's investigation of Wieland's art and ideology, but also for the larger question of how the visual arts in 1960s Canada reflected a forced construction of nationalist identity. In particular, Holmes explores the gendered implications of Wieland's quilt as well as her work more generally, which challenged the nationalist narrative prevalent in Trudeau's Just Society. While Trudeau's nation-remaking project may have attempted to appropriate Wieland's feminist work in its liberal (and male-centred) conception of citizenship, Holmes's piece provides a more nuanced postnationalist approach to understanding the interplay between the philosopher king Trudeau and his concepts of citizenship, and the feminist artist Wieland and her work.

While Trudeau stands tall as a symbol of the Sixties in Canada, it is clear that the politics of the period came in many forms. There were gendered, linguistic, racial, personal, class, local, provincial, and a host of other perspectives, along with the national discourse epitomized by Trudeau. Moreover, while much of the political history of the Sixties has been focused on the proclaimed (B)ig (Q)uestions of (N)ational (P)olitics and (P)olicy, the decade offers intriguing insights into issues that bridge elements of social history and the political. For instance, Christopher Dummitt's article, "A Crash Course in Manhood: Men, Cars, and Risk in Postwar Vancouver," takes up the theme of gender running through Early's and Holmes's work to examine driving, along with postwar ideas about the automobile, as a way of exploring changing notions of masculinity. Dummitt shows how the potentates of the Vancouver Traffic and Safety Council unquestioningly linked notions of what constituted a "good" driver with what made up the "ideal" modern man. However, the construction of postwar modernism built on a foundation of automobile idealism was challenged in the Sixties.

City-beautiful advocates such as Jane Jacobs questioned the utility of the car in the urban landscape, while detractors of unsafe automotive technology such as Ralph Nader unrepentantly challenged the mighty car companies themselves. In this way, Dummitt's article intersects and explains the collision of so many Sixties images: cars, urban development, modernism, and the political discourse of masculinity. Drug use is another enduring image of the Sixties. A staple of the counterculture scene from the Beatniks to the psychedelic excesses of the 1969 Woodstock free love and music festival, drug use also had a political component. Marcel Martel explores one aspect of the politics of pot in his article on the prevention and control of drug use undertaken by the Ontario and Quebec governments during the cultural zenith of recreational drug use. In understanding the comparative responses of the professional health communities and governments on either side of the Ontario-Quebec border, Martel provides insight into how and why each provincial state developed particular agencies and strategies to deal with the high incidence of drug use among the youth of central Canada. In the Sixties the state seemed to take a far more interventionist approach to the nation's drug use than it did in its response to sexual matters.

At the very height of the Sixties counterculture, a relic of old world *real politik* suddenly emerged in Canada like an apparition from the past. The arrival of French President Charles de Gaulle during Canada's Expo '67 celebration in Montreal provides the setting for Olivier Courteaux's examination of one instance of the period's "Big-P" politics. Not surprisingly, it centres on de Gaulle's dramatic and (in)famous declaration from the balcony of Montreal City Hall, "Vive le Québec Libre!" One of the seminal political events of the decade, de Gaulle's intervention provoked a diplomatic row and set off a nationalist firestorm in a Quebec that was already in the throes of a slow-motion explosion. Courteaux shows how the general's fascination with history – France's history in America – merged with France's postcolonial geopolitical aspirations in the Sixties to produce the stirring and provocative declaration which, to this day, still generates heated debate.

As memorable as the protests and the politics were, the period cannot be understood apart from its eclectic and convention-challenging style. Undeniably, architectural unorthodoxy was part of the style of the Sixties. Irreverent postmodern styles came to personify a new-found confidence in Canadian cityscapes such as those of Montreal and Toronto, which became the focus of the modernist architectural movement in Canada. But as France Vanlaethem's piece points out, below the towering new skylines of the country raged a debate over the very nature of Canadian architectural culture. While it looked as though modernism had captured the architectural profession in Canada, Vanlaethem shows that an undercurrent of criticism also marked architectural discourse, especially in the spirited architectural press. As with so many other movements in the decade, the reality of the Sixties did not always match the images we recall so fondly.

Architects were not alone in reshaping the urban fabric in the quickly changing decade. Cities became the epicentre of a potent and burgeoning artistic scene, which merged with the protest and politics of the period to generate a host of new approaches to the visual arts and urban planning. In "Art and Urban Renewal: MOMA's New City Exhibition and Halifax's Uniacke Square," Krys Verrall brings together a number of disciplines to examine the linkages between art, urban renewal, race, and politics in Halifax and New York in the Sixties. Cross-border approaches to public art and urban planning tell us much of the differing attitudes towards poverty, race, and civil rights – not unexpected, given the obvious differences between Halifax (a peripheral city with a small black population) and New York (the epicentre of American, and black American, culture). Yet Verrall also points to many interesting and unexpected similarities in each city's approach towards art and urban renewal.

Finally, it is wise to remember that although the Sixties are emerging as a subject of historical inquiry, they are still too recent to be extricated completely from the realm of memory. The collection's final piece revives Chambers's reminiscent tone and once again reminds us that, as in Verrall's piece, Canadians were indeed part of larger North American trends. Nicholas Olsberg's "California Casual: Selling the Slouch" lyrically tells how California's postwar consumer and commuter-driven influence spread like the tentacles of Los Angeles's sprawling highway system, shaping not only movies, clothing styles, and architectural tastes but also the very meaning of formality in daily life. Olsberg begins his essay as a personal memoir of the period, taking the reader back to a moment of pregnant possibility, when he arrived in North America as a young graduate student. From there, he unfolds the fabric of California's contribution to North American style, the weft and warp of his article bringing the reader along with him as he helps us understand how the permutations of the state's climate, culture, and coolness gripped the Sixties and defined notions of fashion, style, and the spirit of the age. While Canada does not feature as part of Olsberg's discussion, it takes little imagination to realize the obvious implications that California style had on Canadian sensibilities by the Sixties.

Originally part of a conference held at the McCord Museum on "The Sixties" in 2003, these essays ultimately show how the Sixties remain a contradictory period – a decade of triumphal failure, of uncertain clarity, and, above all else, of ambiguous legacy.

NOTES

1 For a good brief view of the meaning of the Sixties, see David Farber, "The Sixties Legacy: 'The Destructive Generation' or 'Years of Hope'?" in *The Columbia Guide to America in the 1960s*, ed. David Farber and Beth Bailey (New York: Columbia University Press, 2001). Some leading American activists from the era have come to the conclusion that the Sixties "had failed them personally and had been a disaster for the country"; they had become disillusioned by the failures in Vietnam, the imperialism of the Soviet regime in the 1970s, and the lost hope of the student and civil rights movements. See, for example, Peter Collier and David Horowitz, eds., *Second Thoughts: Former Radicals Look Back at the Sixties* (New York: Lantham, Md: Madison Books, 1989), xi.

2 The "meaning" of the Sixties is obviously different for Canadians and Americans. American scholar Morris Dickstein has written, "Though many of the events of the decade belong to another world – to a raucous party that lasted long but ended badly – the sixties remain a tangible myth, a set of burnished memories, a point of departure for every kind of social argument, as well as the source of values widely diffused throughout our culture. Some revolutions fail by succeeding; this one seemed to succeed by failing." For Canadians, however, their revolutions were on a different scale (at least outside Quebec), so the lens through which

the era is examined is, from the outset, a different one. See Morris Dickstein, "After Utopia: The 1960s Today" in *Sights on the Sixties*, ed. Barbara L. Tischler (New Brunswick, NJ: Rutgers University Press, 1992).

3 Some have referred to the "High Sixties" as the period between 1964 and 1968. Still others are not so sure just where the "decade" begins or ends. In her introduction to *Sights on the Sixties*, editor Barbara L. Tischler lists the number of ways that the Sixties could be periodized:

1954–1973: Vietnam

1954–1966: The Civil Rights Movement

1966–1969: Black Power, the Formative Years

1960–1968: Camelot and the Great Society

1957–1969: Technology Ascendant

1964–1984: The New Feminism and Women's Liberation

1963–1972: The Beatles to the Beat

Of course, Canadians might periodize their own Sixties history quite differently. An analogous yet obviously incomplete Canadian list might look like this:

1960–1970: Quiet Revolution in Quebec, from Lesage to the October Crisis

1963–1968: Pearson and State Formation (Canada Pension Plan, National Health Care, Flag)

1963–1974: The Years of Economic Nationalism, from Gordon to NDP influence

1968–1982: Trudeau and the Rights Revolution, from the Bedrooms of the Nation to the Charter.

4 There is interesting (if not always scholarly) work being done on all of these themes. On the flag, see Rick Archbold, *I Stand for Canada: The Story of the Maple Leaf Flag* (Toronto: Macfarlane, Walter & Ross, 2002). On Expo '67, Pierre Berton's *1967: The Last Good Year* (Toronto; Macfarlane, Walter & Ross, 1998) provides a lively look at the decade and its discontents. The death of Pierre Elliott Trudeau in 2000 generated an outpouring of nostalgia for the sentiment created by this charismatic politician in 1968. See, for instance, Nancy Southam, ed., *Pierre: Colleagues and Friends Talk about the Trudeau They Knew* (Toronto: McClelland & Stewart, 2005); *Trudeau Albums* (Toronto: McClelland & Stewart, 2000). For more scholarly approaches to Trudeau's legacy written before his death, see Stephen Clarkson, "Charisma and Contradiction: The Legacy of Pierre Elliott Trudeau," *Queen's Quarterly* 107, no.4 (2000), and Andrew Cohen, ed., *Trudeau's Shadow: The Life and Legacy of Pierre Elliott Trudeau* (Toronto: Random House Canada, 1998).

5 For an analysis of the writing of Quebec history and the Sixties, see Ronald Rudin, *Making History in Twentieth-Century Quebec* (Toronto: University of Toronto Press, 1997).

6 In her *Long Way from Home: The Sixties Generation in Canada* (Toronto: Lorimer, 1980), Myrna Kostash comments on the U.S. influence in shaping the Canadian Sixties experience: "The power of American events and personalities of the period is not to be denied – it was felt throughout the world – inasmuch as the centrality of the American *imperium* is not to be denied ... At the same time, of course, the two national experiences are not unrelated" xii.

7 Women's history works in this period include Joy Parr, ed., *A Diversity of Women: Ontario, 1945–1980* (Toronto: Lorimer, 1996); Valerie Korinek, *Roughing It in the Suburbs: Reading Chatelaine Magazine in the Fifties and Sixties* (Toronto: University of Toronto Press, 2000). On students and protest, see Douglas Owram, *Born at the Right Time: A History of the Baby Boom Generation* (Ottawa: University of Ottawa Press, 1996), especially chapter 9, "Youth Radicalism in the Sixties". On native issues, including the Sixties, see J.R. Miller, *Skyscrapers Hide the Heavens: A History of Indian-White Relations in Canada* (Toronto: University of Toronto Press, 2000).

8 Some of the better-known American treatments of the period include Todd Gitlin's *The Sixties: Years of Hope, Days of Rage* (New York: Bantam Books, 1993); John Blum, *Years of Discord: American Politics and Society, 1961–1974* (New York: W.W. Norton, 1991); David Farber, *Age of Great Dreams: America in the 1960s* (New York: Hill, 1994). International comparisons can be found in Arthur Marwick, *The Sixties: Social and Cultural Transformation in Britain, France, Italy, and the United States, 1958–1974* (New York: Oxford University Press, 1998). For an assessment of new works and historiographic analyses of the era, see, for instance, M.J. Neale, "The Sixties as History: A Review of the Political Historiography," *Reviews in American History* 33, no. 1 (2005): 133–52; Andrew Hunt, "'When Did the Sixties Happen?' Searching for New Directions," *Journal of Social History* 33, no. 1 (1999): 147–61. Some observers, such as political commentator David Frum, have challenged the view that the Sixties were a watershed decade, and have argued that the 1970s have actually been more significant in the postwar period; see his *How We Got Here: The 70's, the Decade That Brought You Modern Life – For Better or Worse* (New York: Basic Books, 2000).

9 For instance, John English, Robert Bothwell, and Ian Drummond's survey of the postwar period, *Canada since 1945* (Toronto: University of

Toronto Press, 1989), elicits little of the passion of the Sixties. Its main section on the era is titled "The Sixties: Nationalism and Culture," and the book deals largely with the partisan politics and economic issues of the period.

10 Kostash's *Long Way from Home* is one of the few early, specifically Canadian works on the Sixties. In it, she rhapsodizes: "I wrote this because I am in love with the Sixties, with the passions and ideas, friendships and loves, music and dance and poetry, stoned highs and sorrows that the period generated. I 'came of age' in 1965: I turned twenty-one, and threw myself into the great learning about camaraderie, war, imperialism, rock 'n' roll, the Godhead, vagabonding, lust, appetite and women power; and I consider myself blessed to have been young in a period when the vision of the good and true was up for grabs" (xiii). For another, more personal, view of the Sixties, see Douglas Fetherling, *Travels by Night: A Memoir of the Sixties* (Toronto: Lester, 1994). See also James Dickerson, ed., *North to Canada: Men and Women against the Vietnam War* (Westport, Conn: Praeger, 1999).

11 Peter C. Newman's *Renegade in Power* (Toronto: McClelland & Stewart, 1963), an "intimate portrait" of John Diefenbaker, was one of the best-selling books of the Sixties, as was George Grant's *Lament for a Nation* (Princeton: Van Nostrand, 1965).

12 Alvin Finkel, *Our Lives: Canada after 1945* (Toronto: University of Toronto Press, 1997); Magda Fahrni and Robert Rutherdale, eds., *Creating Postwar Canada: Community, Diversity, and Dissent, 1945–1975* (Vancouver: University of British Columbia Press, 2006). Good new work on the 1950s includes Nancy Christie and Michael Gauvreau, eds., *Cultures of Citizenship in Post-war Canada, 1940–1955* (Montreal & Kingston: McGill-Queen's University Press, 2004).

13 Cyril Levitt, *Children of Privilege: Student Revolt in the Sixties: A Study of Student Movements in Canada, the United States, and West Germany* (Toronto: University of Toronto Press, 1984).

14 On Rochdale College, see David Sharpe, *Rochdale: The Runaway College* (Toronto: Anansi, 1987). On the student counterculture, see Owram, *Born at the Right Time*, chapter 8: "'Hope I Die before I Get Old': The Rise of the Counter Culture, 1963–1968," and Ron Verzuh, *Underground Times: Canada's Flower-Child Revolutionaries* (Toronto: Deneau, 1989). On student protest in Saskatchewan, see James M. Pitsula, "Cicero versus Socrates: The Liberal Arts Debate in the 1960s at the University of Saskatchewan, Regina Campus," *Historical Studies in Education* 15, no. 1 (2003), and "Competing Ideals: Athletics and Stu-

dent Radicalism at the University of Saskatchewan, Regina Campus, in the 1960s and 1970s," *Sport History Review* 34, no. 1 (2003).

15 As Steve Hewitt has pointed out, Canadian campuses also became a focus of state security agencies during the Sixties. See his *Spying 101: The RCMP's Secret Activities at Canadian Universities, 1917–1997* (Toronto: University of Toronto Press, 2002).

16 Gregory Albo, "Canada, Left-Nationalism, and Younger Voices," *Studies in Political Economy* 33 (1990); Gilbert Levine, "The Waffle and the Labour Movement," *Studies in Political Economy* 33 (1990); Varda Burstyn, "The Waffle and the Women's Movement," *Studies in Political Economy* 33 (1990); John Bullen, "The Ontario Waffle and the Struggle for an Indepdendent Socialist Canada: Conflict within the NDP," *Canadian Historical Review* 64, no. 2 (1983).

17 See, for instance, Stephen Azzi, *Walter Gordon and the Rise of Canadian Nationalism* (Montreal & Kingston: McGill-Queen's University Press, 1999).

18 Recent work on the Quiet Revolution and Quebec includes Yves Bélanger, Robert Comeau, and Céline Métivier, eds., *La Révolution Tranquille: 40 Ans Plus Tard: Un Bilan* (Montreal: YLB Editeur, 2000); Kenneth McRoberts, *Misconceiving Canada: The Struggle for National Unity* (Toronto: Oxford University Press, 1997); Gilles Paquet, *Oublier la Révolution tranquille* (Montreal: Liber, 2000). A new view of Quebec's political and economic model can be found in Michel Venne, ed., *Vive Quebec! New Thinking and New Approaches to the Quebec Nation* (Toronto: Lorimer, 2001).

19 For the Acadian awakening in the Sixties, see Michel Cormier, *Louis J. Robichaud: A Not So Quiet Revolution* (Moncton, NB: Saye, 2002). A recent look that challenges traditional understandings of multiculturalism in Canadian history is Richard Day's *Multiculturalism and the History of Canadian Diversity* (Toronto: Lorimer, 2000).

20 John Hagan, *Northern Passage: American Vietnam War Resisters in Canada* (Cambridge, Mass: Harvard University Press, 2001); Frank Kusch, *All American Boys: Draft Dodgers in Canada from the Vietnam War* (Westport, Conn.: Praeger, 2002); David Churchill, "An Ambiguous Welcome: Vietnam Draft Resistance, the Canadian State, and Cold War Containment," *Histoire Sociale/Social History* 37 (2004).

2

The Sixties in Print: Remembering Quebec's Quiet Revolution

GRETTA CHAMBERS

The Sixties are far enough behind us to make for a wide variety of hindsights; at the same time, they have not yet been historically classified and filed. As a society we have grown out of this decade, but it left an indelible mark on those of us who were young (or not so young) adults during those heady years of infinite possibility. This was particularly true of the Sixties as they were lived in Quebec. Anyone who was at university at that time had his or her view of higher education abruptly changed forever. Anyone interested in politics had his or her relationship to the political process dramatically altered. Our awareness of society as a framework for action rather than simply as the passive locus of belonging was sudden and very heady. For Quebecers, the Sixties represent a clean break with the past. And for a moment in our history, no matter what the past we were breaking with, our hopes for the future were remarkably consensual.

o—o—o

We did not arrive at all these political and social discoveries by ourselves. We were part of the great upheavals that swept through the Western world. We, too, were affected by a widespread rejection of the 1940s wartime philosophy and a refusal to shoulder the postwar conservatism of the 1950s and the accompanying couldn't-care-less attitude of the young, who were spoiled by an economic revival to which they had not contributed. The style adopted as the 1960s dawned was one of daring. One could – indeed, one should – try everything. Nothing was sacred, including continuity. Particularly for the young, the self-assertion that grew out of this movement to break out of the existing social, political, and cultural constraints was both heady and contagious.

Here in Quebec, we were spared the civil unrest and violence that gripped some European societies. In France, the rise of the radical student movement, aimed at breaking out of the straitjacket of a university system that dated back to Napoleonic times, culminated in the demonstrations and riots of 1968. While the extent of such agitation and ferment was not visited on us, the echoes of that revolt were heard here, where the university network could not accommodate the young Quebecers who were now clamouring to be allowed entrance to post-secondary education. There was no room for them in Quebec's institutions of higher learning. In growing numbers they denounced the injustice of being deprived of their right to education.

The result of these rumblings of discontent was the movement "McGill français," which generated a massive demonstration demanding that McGill University be opened to Quebec's French-speaking youth. The McGill campus was shaken for some time. In the end, however, this Sixties phenomenon had a very happy outcome – it turned out to be the catalyst for the foundation of the Université du Québec and for college networks across the province, thus knocking postsecondary education unceremoniously off its elitist pedestal.

When one thinks back to those days, it is still hard to explain how centuries-old habits and customs vanished almost overnight. At the time, no one mourned their passing. The questions came later and centred around what had emerged to replace them. In five years, Quebec's churches were emptied and the "priest-ridden" society disappeared without a trace. A public education system was put in place and the *collège classique* and clergy-run schools became things of the past. Quebec set up a permanent and professional civil service that no longer depended on political appointments from top to bottom.

On the cultural front, we never matched the Beatles, but we did produce our own popular irreverents who changed the world of Quebec music and entertainment. In 1968 the fast-paced musical review *L'Ostidshow* broke the mold of cultural correctness, and its *chansonniers* and entertainers – Robert Charlebois, Yvon Deschamps, Louise Forestier, and Mouffe – not only became the rage but set the stage for the rest of the century. The 1950s had brought us television; in the 1960s, homegrown showbiz came into its own.

Although we were sloughing off taboos, values, beliefs and traditions that had ruled the social model on which our society had been run for generations, we were also waking up to the existence of a physical heritage that needed both appreciation and protection. Not until the mid-Sixties was Old Montreal recognized as a historic site to be protected. By then, of course, Quebec and particularly Montreal were in the grip of a development boom that would provide an impressive heritage of its own. Place Ville Marie, imposing as it was above ground, was groundbreaking as the beginning of an underground city. But the crowning glory of the decade was undoubtedly Expo '67. It is still an image to be conjured with. The event itself – the buildings, the site, its very existence – was a most powerful symbol of Quebec's energy, momentum and potential. One cannot exaggerate the effect of Expo on people of my generation. We were as though reborn.

The era has passed whether we like it or not. But for a Quebecer like myself, who turned forty in 1967, there was a newfound confidence, optimism, and tangible proof that we were capable, as a society, of becoming first-class citizens of the twentieth century. With all but unlimited horizons and quite capable of pulling off any project within our means, this belief became an article of faith that it has been difficult to shed.

The whole concept of *Maître chez nous*, the huge success of Expo, and the excitement that rippled through society gave Quebecers, both English- and French-speaking, the feeling that they all had a stake in what looked and felt like an open-ended future. Looking back, it is clear that much of the aura of success was deceptive. Expo sparked the imaginations of more than just Quebecers and Canadians, encouraging countless people to surpass themselves. For instance, scores of designers from around the world descended on us, plying their ideas in what they saw as an opening market of innovation and experimentation. Most of them did not stay. We were not ready to follow the Expo star in any concerted way. Our euphoria denoted a frame of mind more than a state of affairs. When the world moved on, we were once more left to face our inward-looking social, economic, and cultural habits alone. They proved more difficult to transcend on our own without the impetus of a grand, overriding design.

The decade itself, of course, generated much physical and verbal violence that was impossible to square with the spirit in which the Sixties had begun. Bombs in mailboxes were signs of disturbing things to come. Much unquiet – indeed visceral, revolutionary tracts and positions – began to surface in literature and publications of all kinds, presaging the October Crisis of 1970.

In the Sixties, as the economy improved and grew, the dominance of the English language and English speakers became more and more evident and resented, paving the way for the linguistic tensions of the following decade. The Sixties, however, did see the end of the linguistic and social compartmentalization of Quebec's written press. In this professionally seminal decade of my journalistic career, I began to research, write, and broadcast a weekly radio program for the CBC that entailed reading 140 Quebec daily and weekly newspapers each week. It was called "The Province in Print," and it lasted for fourteen years. When it began in the Sixties there were fourteen dailies; there are now eight. But in those original fourteen there was a distinct demarcation between French and English, urban and rural; the city papers did not deal with the same news as their rural counterparts; as for the French-English dichotomy, front-page stories could have been reporting on events in different countries, depending on the language in which they were published.

By the end of the decade the francophone press had not appreciably changed its attitude, but anglophone newspapers had become more aware of, sensitive to, and even interested in the political and social evolution of the society in which the communities they served were rooted. Meanwhile, the urban-rural split was even more marked. City papers, French and English, both talked "city talk." By the end of the decade, television had taken over the regions as surely as it dominated the cities, and the urban-rural dichotomy was beginning to blur. Local issues continued to dominate the regional press, but the discrepancies in the decisions about what constituted news were less evident. As Quebec's social and political realities began to fuse into a catch-all that became known as "Quebec's superior interests," the province's press took up the mantra of the "Quebec model."

If you read 140 newspapers a week, you become a "resource person," so I did the rounds of election-night broadcasts, beginning with the provincial election of 1966. My perusal of the regional press convinced me that Jean Lesage's Liberals – that legendary *équipe de tonnere*, were going to lose. Try telling that to any big-city reporter, French or English, at the time! Whenever I timidly tried out my thesis, I was reminded gently but categorically that I had not been covering the political scene for very long. So on that first election night I was too intimidated to trot out my theories, gleaned from the regional press. Afterwards I was furious with myself for not having trusted my research, which of course turned out to be dead on. Lesage lost and the Union Nationale under Daniel Johnson swept back into power. I learned a valuable lesson from the experience – that the ideas embraced by the Quiet Revolution, which had captured the imagination of urbanized Quebecers and become very much part of their political and economic thinking, had only just started to take hold in the regions.

The Quiet Revolution came to an inconclusive end with the radical change of government. It did not, however, simply fade away. It lived on as a defining moment in Quebec's modern historical memory. Even new arrivals, immigrants who have come to Quebec since the Sixties, quickly become marked by the indelible vestiges of Quiet Revolution values. This home truth was born out when Jean Charest, at the beginning of his career with the Quebec Liberal Party, suggested that the Quiet Revolution had done its time as Quebec's indigenous economic model and should henceforth be replaced with something more modern. His statement landed like a bomb, and howls of protest came from left and right. Charest had touched a sensitive chord across society, even among those who were too young to have much idea of what the Quiet Revolution had been about when it was at work changing the old political and economic order.

The concept of the Quiet Revolution – and the state interventionism on which it based Quebec's economic development – has by now acquired a mystical legitimacy that is not to be confused with the substance of contemporary political and economic policy. It is often difficult today to hitch the liberating philosophy on which the "revolution" was based to the needs of a modern economy. In the Sixties, economic development was also the goal. But how could Quebec begin to shape its own economic destiny when all the economic levers were owned and controlled by other people's capital? The only source of indigenous capital was the state pension funds, which generated the birth of the Caisse de dépôt et placement. The rest is history. The question today is not whether state intervention was required to jumpstart Quebec Inc. forty years ago. What is now being asked is whether that necessarily means that Quebec must rely forever on state intervention to generate economic development.

In fact, if we had truly learned from the Sixties, we would now understand that, to succeed, it is important not to be a slave to the gospels of the past. A policy is good and productive, not on the basis of its conformity with what has gone before but on whether it is tailored to reach an objective in the present that looks towards the future.

The Quiet Revolution is not to be discounted today. It was of its time. At the beginning of the Sixties, Quebec was far behind; by the end, it had not only caught up but was moving ahead at a good clip. Taking a chance, breaking new ground, was definitely the style of the day, and it led to such substantive social change that remembering it for whatever reason can be salutary and even morale boosting, as long as our memories do not lose track of our mindset during those years. That is what made them special.

o——o——o

The entire Western world was marked by the Sixties. But for us here in Quebec, for so long kept on the fringes of North American social and economic development, this decade represents a turning point that restored us to the bosom of the geographical, economic, political, social, and cultural world in which we live as actors in our own right. Roch Carrier, well before he became a public figure and the custodian of our national culture – when he was known and listened to as a writer and author of such books as *La Guerre, Yes Sir!* and *The Hockey Sweater and Other Stories*, summed up the Sixties as "la petite révolution tranquille qui a permis à notre société de passer du

17e siècle à l'avant garde du 20e siècle presque du jour au lendemain" (The peaceful little revolution that allowed our society to pass from the seventeenth to the twentieth centuries, almost from one day to the next).

A bit of dialogue from the old vaudeville act "Mister Gallagher, Mister Shine" goes like this:

"Do you remember?"

"Yes, I remember."

"Then you're much older than I."

Like Quebec's motto, *Je me souviens*, I do remember.

3

Canadian Women and the International Arena in the Sixties: The Voice of Women/La voix des femmes and the Opposition to the Vietnam War

FRANCES EARLY

The Voice of Women/La voix des femmes (VOW) was born out of rage and hope. The five thousand women who flocked to VOW's banner in the months following its founding in Toronto's Massey Hall on 28 July 1960 sought to combat the popular impression that nothing could be done to prevent the drift towards nuclear war. VOW members insisted that nuclear disarmament was possible and pressed home the point that Canada could pursue an independent foreign policy that rejected the legitimacy of nuclear weapons as instruments of war. Buoyed up by the rising tide of a worldwide "Ban the Bomb" movement, VOW had some success lobbying government and educating the public about the dangers of nuclear war and the health and environmental hazards associated with nuclear weapons testing. In concert with other peace groups, VOW helped to influence the U.S. and Soviet heads of state to sign the Partial Nuclear Test Ban Treaty in 1963. Flush with this victory, VOW engaged in specific activities to bring home to North Americans the human cost of the United States' prosecution of the Vietnam War. At the same time, VOW members defined peace broadly to encompass social justice issues; during the Sixties the group sparked significant debate in Canada about bilingualism and biculturalism and worked to end racial discrimination in specific communities, notably Halifax, Nova Scotia, an area with a significant

African Canadian population.[1] VOW also initiated a plan for a world peace year that resulted in the United Nations' designation of 1965 as International Cooperation Year.

At its inception, VOW served as a lightning rod for women's discontent with Cold War politics and helped bring into open debate women's marginalized civic role within the nation. Initially, the association's presentation of its members as serious-minded and responsible mother-citizens secured VOW a public hearing for its views. This apparently transparent and non-threatening public identity of VOW members as civic-minded homemakers dovetailed with an unbroken record of Canadian women's twentieth-century maternalist social reform and peace work. But because VOW grouped women together to challenge the male-dominant structures and values associated with militarism and war making, and rapidly absorbed the militant spirit and goals of a burgeoning and tumultuously left-leaning social protest movement, the organization eventually lost favour in the public eye. VOW's cogent criticism of Prime Minister Lester Pearson's decision in 1963 to accept nuclear weapons for Canada, and the arrest of prominent VOW leaders Thérèse Casgrain and Kay Macpherson in Paris while attempting to deliver a letter to the secretary general of NATO, led many Canadians by mid-decade to view VOW members with suspicion.

In consequence, VOW's membership decreased. In the latter part of the Sixties, its leaders found themselves guiding a smaller but more resilient and focused organization of peace activists into a new era of social protest that was strongly influenced by the emergence of second-wave feminism. Beyond Canada's borders, coteries of women peace activists, including groups in the United States (New England), England, Scotland, and New Zealand, found inspiration in the work of the Voice of Women and assumed the Canadian group's name and objectives.[2]

In this essay I take up the story of VOW's opposition to the Vietnam War in the heady atmosphere of the politicized 1960s. After providing a brief overview of the organization's evolving perspective on the war, I elaborate on three specific anti-war projects which the group sponsored: first, sending a VOW leader, Kay Macpherson, to North

Vietnam to witness and report on destruction and death at the war front; second, assisting in a humanitarian knitting project on behalf of North and South Vietnamese children caught in combat zones; and third, sponsoring a trip of women from North and South Vietnam to Canada and arranging for U.S. peace activists to meet with them on Canadian soil. These activities, I shall suggest, contributed to Canadian anti-war sentiments and stimulated a commitment among ordinary citizens in all provinces to provide humanitarian aid to Vietnam. VOW's creative anti-war projects helped to shape how the North American peace movement came to articulate its indictment of the United States' prosecution of the Vietnam War. I shall also explore how VOW members conceptualized their anti-war work. I hope to demonstrate that members shared the conviction that exposing "the pain of others," particularly in relation to the "knowing" woman's body, strengthened the resolve of Canadian citizens, notably women, to develop a critical perspective on their own government's de facto support of U.S. war policy in Vietnam.[3]

In June 1964, two months before the United States Senate passed the Tonkin Gulf Resolution – a document which came to be seen as a virtual declaration of war against North Vietnam – the VOW annual meeting passed its own resolution on the Vietnam imbroglio: "Whereas the political and military situation in South Vietnam is steadily deteriorating; be it resolved that the Canadian Government be urged to use its influence in a reconvened Geneva Conference toward the demilitarization and neutralization under international guarantees of Cambodia, Laos, and Vietnam." In February 1965, the same month that U.S. President Lyndon Johnson ordered intensive bombing of strategic targets in North Vietnam, VOW president Kay Macpherson reported to members that VOW was sending a delegation to meet with Prime Minister Lester Pearson and representatives of the embassies of the United States, the Soviet Union, Great Britain, India, France, and Poland to urge a ceasefire, the reconvening of the Geneva Conference, and a speedy peace settlement for Vietnam. Six members of the delegation (which numbered more than fifty) ended up meeting not the prime minister but Paul Martin, Sr, the secretary of state for external affairs. These six women found the outcome disappointing, and a VOW report commented, "Mr. Martin very diplomatically had not replied to our suggestion for immediate cease-fire in Vietnam, nor did we feel that Canada was preparing any bold initiative for peace."[4]

Six months later, VOW members received a report from President Kay Macpherson that included one full page of basic information about the Vietnam War. Entitled "Vietnam and You," the document was subtitled: "Where is Vietnam?" "Why did the United States enter Vietnam?" "Who is fighting in Vietnam?" "How does the United States justify fighting in Vietnam?" When will the war be over?" and, finally, "What has it to do with me?" With regard to this last question, the answer presented the VOW view – influenced by the organization's involvement from its inception in the international "Ban the Bomb" movement – that the war in Vietnam represented a struggle between the United States and China that could escalate into a nuclear and global war. "Canada, as an American frontier," the document stated, "would be bombed in such a war as surely as the countryside around Saigon is being bombed now. No home between Halifax and Vancouver will be immune." Members were urged to "write to the Prime Minister, President [Lyndon] Johnson, their member of Parliament, to Canadian and American newspapers, [and] to speak out for an end to American fighting in Vietnam."[5]

During the next ten years, until the formal cessation of hostilities in Vietnam in 1975, VOW was consistent and persistent in its efforts to help end the war. The organization sent numerous delegations to Ottawa, lobbied government officials, sought to educate Canadian citizens about the war through a variety of educative means, and participated actively in all manner of anti-war projects and events. Further, VOW established effective communication with American and international women's peace movements, attending numerous conferences and sponsoring some meetings on Canadian soil.[6] VOW also developed a special working relationship with Women Strike for Peace (WSP), a feisty and formidable grassroots group founded in the United States in 1961, one year after VOW's formation.[7]

o—o—o

Turning now to a consideration of the first of the three special projects mentioned in my introduction, in 1967 VOW endorsed a plan for Kay Macpherson, VOW president from 1963 to 1967, to visit North Vietnam. Invited by the Hanoi-based Union des femmes, Macpherson accepted the dangerous mission so that she could report back to Canadians about the devastation the war had wrought. Because of the massive U.S. bombing of Hanoi and other areas in North Vietnam in late 1967, the Vietnamese women's group requested that Macpherson and the other members of the delegation delay their trip. Hence, Macpherson actually arrived for a two-week visit to North Vietnam in June 1968, a month in which marginally fewer U.S. bombs were dropped than in previous months.

When Macpherson accepted the Vietnamese women's invitation she was just completing her term as VOW president and was relocating for a sabbatical year in Cambridge, England, with her husband, political theorist C.B. Macpherson. Assuming in October 1967 that she would be departing for North Vietnam within a few days, she penned an eloquent reflection on her reasons for accepting the invitation of the Union des femmes. Macpherson was well aware of the danger she and two other delegates were facing, and she intended her text to be used for political ends, as VOW leaders saw fit:

In case I get to Hanoi and end up with a bomb on top of me
I want to put down one or two thoughts beforehand ... I hope
to be able to explain to other people how it must feel to be a
woman in Vietnam today. Perhaps if we can understand this
better it will make it impossible for us to forget, to ignore or to
stand aside while these terrible things are happening to people
like us ...
    I suppose I am going to Hanoi for publicity and if what I say
doesn't have too much effect, perhaps if I should get killed then
it would have more effect ... If it is hard to imagine these things
happening to hundreds of women we have never known, perhaps when it happens to someone closer to us, to one of us, it
can become more real. Perhaps then we will resolve to do some-

thing about changing this dreadful situation ... It's very simple, and very difficult, but it is well worth living and dying for.[8]

In this passage, Macpherson employs text to conceptualize her body as an imagined subject in a combat zone. She articulates for herself and for her intended readers – VOW members residing in safety in Canada – the symbolic significance of a possibly broken and dead Western woman's body at ground zero in an Asian and, in the context of the times, Orientalized theatre of war. Historian Wendy Parkins, in her study of the British suffrage movement, has elucidated instances where women's bodies become sites of political struggle, and her insight may be related to Macpherson's textual strategy in this instance. Pertinent, too, is a related comment by Parkins: "Where the specificities of female embodiment have been grounds for exclusion or diminished participation, deliberately drawing attention to their bodies has been an important strategy for women engaged in dissident citizenship. Such dissidents have understood their embodiment not as a limitation but as a means by which the parameters of the political domain could be contested."[9]

Macpherson and other VOW members shared the conviction that women's bodies could be employed effectively in such actions as visits to war zones to underscore the tragic loss of civilian lives in Vietnam; they sought to communicate to the general public the futility and senselessness of military strategies that haphazardly resulted in massive civilian casualties. Thus, two years before Macpherson's visit to North Vietnam, VOW had embraced a bold project that exploited, at the same time that it recast, the powerful iconic image of a maternal figure knitting in wartime for "her boys." VOW elected to knit items of clothing for the victimized Orientalized Other: Vietnamese children residing at the warfront.

This decision to engage in what was commonly understood to be women's traditional wartime work – namely, knitting – to spread an anti-war message by supporting civilians rather than soldiers in the field, was inspired by the work of a Vancouver-based humanitarian group, Canadian Aid for Vietnam Civilians (CAVC). On 17 February 1966, fifty-five individuals representing a broad cross-section of the community, including physicians, lawyers, literary figures, community leaders, and prominent spokespersons for peace, had come together with the common goal of launching a campaign to provide medical aid in the form of supplies and funding for civilians in Vietnam. CAVC's mission was to work to establish friendship and understanding between Canada and Vietnam, to help Canadians become acquainted with the horrors of the war, and to support sincere efforts to bring the war to a speedy conclusion. CAVC's founders also pledged to work for the implementation of the 1954 Geneva Agreements, including free elections in Vietnam. Five months later, in July, a children's committee of CAVC was established that specifically identified the needs of Vietnamese children caught in the crossfire of war.[10]

Sheila Young, an ardent peace activist who belonged to the Vancouver chapter of the Women's International League for Peace and Freedom (WILPF) and served on the executive of CAVC, directed the children's committee from its inception in early 1966 until it ceased its activities a decade later. Young had close ties with the British Medical Aid Committee, which had initiated a knitting plan for Vietnamese children in 1965. Although CAVC, as well as the British Medical Aid Committee, respected the Vietnamese request that humanitarian help come chiefly in the form of medical supplies and money, Young initiated a knitting project to provide clothing for Vietnamese children as a means of communicating the harsh realities of war; she hoped thereby to influence ordinary citizens across North America to press for a speedy end to the war. By November 1966, just a few months after the establishment of CAVC's children's committee, the knitting project had gained momentum. In a letter to Kay Macpherson, Young asserted, "We have found that actual involvement in 'making things' has done more to arouse compassion and publicize the great need for acts of humanitarianism, and the desperate need to halt the war, than any other project."[11]

Lil Greene, an active VOW member residing in Toronto, read of the children's committee's activities in a CAVC bulletin and soon afterwards organized the Ontario VOW Knitting Project for Vietnamese Children. Describing its beginnings, she used militant maternalist language that brought attention to children's fragile bodies to explain why Voices, as VOW members called themselves, had assumed this particular kind of humanitarian work: "We began really because the thought of a child burned by napalm, a child riddled or maimed with shrapnel or bomb fragments; such a child without care, even the warmth of a cot blanket or a knitted vest, perhaps as we saw in the Special Edition of *Ramparts* magazine ... wrapped in newspapers ... all this was too much to bear, without acting to ease the pain ... of the child, and in our own hearts."[12]

Within one year, the Ontario chapter of VOW reported that Greene had about five hundred Ontario women, most of whom were not VOW members, knitting garments in dark colours. These items were sent to CAVC in Vancouver, to be taken to Vietnam on a Soviet ship. Knitters in Toronto included members of the United Jewish People's Order, the Canadian Friends Service Committee, and the Quaker-run Elizabeth Fry Sisterhood. Further afield, knitters included women of the United Church West Ellesmere Women's Group and the Ladies Auxiliaries of the Mine, Mill and Smelter Workers Union of Sudbury, Timmins, and Port Arthur. Young girls, too, contributed knitted items by virtue of their membership in the Girl Guides or Canadian Girls in Training (an offspring of the Young Women's Christian Association).

It was largely as a result of the mandate of the CAVC children's committee and the Ontario VOW knitting project that the VOW national office decided in early 1967 to concentrate on the plight of children in Vietnam. At a council meeting in Toronto in January, Ann Gertler, a member of the Quebec branch of VOW, reported being in touch with Helen Frumin, the executive secretary of the U.S. Committee of Responsibility, whose members were mostly physicians. Frumin had informed Gertler that "the only thing that has any impact on the State Department in Washington is the napalmed children." At this meeting, VOW decided to form a project to inform Canadian physicians of its concern about injured and at-risk Vietnamese children. Council members also chose to inform VOW branches that an article entitled "Children of Vietnam" by William F. Pepper of Mercy College in Dobbs Ferry, New York, which had just appeared in *Ramparts* magazine, would be sent to every member of parliament. An accompanying letter would urge MPs to do what they could to end the bombing in Vietnam and to aid suffering civilians in all areas of the country, North as well as South.[13]

In 1967, as individuals across Canada learned more about humanitarian efforts to ease the suffering of civilians in Vietnam, the knitting project sponsored by CAVC and Ontario VOW attracted increasing numbers of volunteer knitters. Some women's groups and individuals contacted CAVC's Sheila Young in Vancouver and sent their knitted garments and blankets to her. Others sent their knitted items to Lil Greene for reshipment to the Vancouver CAVC office. All the knitters understood why the garments had to be produced in dark colours: children living in combat zones required camouflage to protect them from U.S. bombs.

By 1969, VOW had established a strong bond with WSP, the maternalist U.S. women's peace movement, which in philosophy and membership shared many features with VOW. Like VOW, it had been formed in the early Sixties to protest nuclear brinkmanship and environmental dangers associated with nuclear bomb testing, and it had since become a creative and leading force in the U.S. anti-war movement.[14] VOW also had close ties with WILPF, the international women's league that had been founded in Europe in 1919, following the First World War, with much support from North American women. WILPF had active chapters in many parts of the United States and in a few Canadian cities, notably Vancouver and Toronto. Women peace workers in VOW, WSP, and WILPF enjoyed close personal ties. Throughout the Sixties, representatives of the three groups crossed paths at a variety of international women's peace conferences in Europe and elsewhere. Voices travelled to the United States to participate in WSP-sponsored events, and U.S. women peace activists crossed the border into Canada to attend VOW conferences.

In such circumstances, it is not surprising that the Canadian-based knitting project attracted U.S. knitters. In 1969 Anne Hardy, a WSP member in Rochester, New York, became the U.S. coordinator of the knitting project. Hardy and Lil Greene communicated with each other frequently, and Hardy arranged for shipments of knitted items to be sent to Greene's home in Toronto so that they could be forwarded to the CAVC office in Vancouver. Leaflets were sent to Hardy for distribution to U.S. knitters listing the kinds of item Vietnamese women had requested and underlining the need for the wool to be in dark shades; patterns were included in some mailings as well as copies of the CAVC children's committee's bulletins. On the U.S. West Coast, WSP member Anna Shiffer headed the L.A. Knitting Circle and was identified by Greene in a letter to Macpherson as "one of our original U.S. knitters." Another Californian, Valida Davila, organized a group in her hometown, Escondido, called Old Dolls for Peace. In correspondence with Greene, Davila commented: "Today distances are no barrier to communication. Knitting and doing other peace work, mostly by mail, keep me from becoming sick with anguish at the horror the people of the United States are [perpetrating] on the Vietnamese ... What a terrible state of moral degradation we, supposed to be the greatest and most powerful nation, have come to."[15]

Both VOW and WSP appreciated how delicate was the task they had assumed of drawing into the knitting project U.S. women who were not active in the anti-war movement but who empathized with and wished to help civilian victims of war. At the same time, many U.S. women felt loyalty to their government and wanted to believe that their country was engaged in a just war. Further, the act of knitting clothing for Vietnamese children could be construed as aiding and abetting the enemy; the U.S. government had the power to prosecute women engaged in such activity under the U.S. Trading with the Enemy Act.

Further difficulties ensued when in 1969 CAVC, which had been distributing its donated goods and funds to Red Cross organizations in both South and North Vietnam, made a policy change, electing to direct clothing and medical supplies solely to the National Liberation Front Red Cross for Children. CAVC officials reasoned that in this manner humanitarian aid would reach the Vietnamese children most in need – those at the centre of intense military engagement. But this decision had ramifications for the knitting project in the United States. Hardy felt obliged to revise the literature she distributed to interested knitters to reflect CAVC's policy shift, and in January 1970 she wrote to Greene that some potential U.S. knitters were now loath to participate in the project.

By this time the knitting project had acquired strong momentum; there were well over two thousand knitters across Canada and several hundred in the United States. Anger in the United States concerning the manner in which the government was prosecuting the Vietnam War kept American women's participation in the knitting project fairly constant. Meanwhile Greene maintained detailed records of each knitter from whom she received donations. Two shoe boxes stuffed with 3" x 5" file cards are included in the VOW papers at the National Archives in Ottawa. These records document the humanitarian work of thousands of ordinary North American citizens who felt compelled to do something to ameliorate the lives of children caught up in the maelstrom of war. In some cases, the cards demonstrate that individuals kept up their knitting for a decade; each record lists each item knitted. The granddaughter of one VOW knitter vividly recalls that she and her siblings and cousins resented the amount of time her apparently non-political grandmother spent knitting "for VOW." Today she is proud of her grandmother's commitment to easing the suffering of powerless victims of war.[16]

As the war dragged on, the variety of knitters increased dramatically, especially in Canada. Church women constituted the majority of knitters, but trade union auxiliaries and service groups, religious and secular, were well represented. The Silver Cross Mothers of Canada, an association of women who had lost their sons in war, committed themselves to the knitting project. Public school students became knitters, organizing young people's groups themselves, and daughters and mothers sometimes knitted together for the project. Some men participated, donating funds or purchasing yarn. A number of yarn manufacturers made generous donations.[17]

The inspired leaders of the knitting project, Sheila Young and Lil Greene, had consciously reformulated the maternal image of a woman knitting during wartime. In this manner, they were following – while at the same time recasting – the maternalist ideology of the women's peace movement of the Sixties. By placing the implicitly motherly woman knitter in the service of the victimized Other, these women and the organizations that sponsored the knitting project, including WSP in the United States, unsettled the standard war story. However, Young and Greene understood that this single project would not affect the duration or outcome of the war in terms of U.S. policy or the Canadian government's acquiescence to and quiet bolstering of the policy. But they appreciated that the reality of a North

American woman knitting for Vietnamese children, especially for children living outside U.S. military control on the war front, challenged people to think critically about the war. In this sense, they perceived knitting to be political work in the service of the larger anti-war movement of the times. Women who spent hours, days, perhaps years, knitting dark-coloured clothing to help camouflage Vietnamese children when they ventured away from their underground shelters were reminded frequently of the pain and suffering of others.

In addition to Kay Macpherson's journey to North Vietnam and VOW's leadership role in the Knitting Project for Vietnamese Children, Voices sponsored a third and related project in protest against the Vietnam War. In 1969, at the height of the bloody conflict, VOW arranged for delegations of women from North Vietnam and the National Liberation Front of South Vietnam to visit Canada to provide personal testimony about the tragic consequences of the war, especially in relation to civilian casualties. Because Canada was not at war with North Vietnam, it was legal for women who were the designated "enemy" in the United States to enter and move around freely in Canada. VOW president Muriel Duckworth, Macpherson's successor, accompanied the Vietnamese women's delegation on their travels across Canada, during which they gave talks and held press conferences concerning the impact of the war on their land.

This summer visit to Canada was not the first time Canadian peace women and women from Vietnam had met to discuss strategies to hasten the end of the war. During the second half of the 1960s, VOW delegates, along with American women representing peace groups in their own polarized country, attended a number of international women's peace conferences at which representatives from Vietnamese women's groups were present. Indeed, much of the planning for the 1969 Vietnamese women's trip to Canada had been arranged at an international gathering of peace women in Paris in 1968. Bringing Vietnamese women to Canada made it possible for many more women, especially American women, to meet with and learn from the purported enemy.

The events and meetings that took place while the Vietnamese women's delegation visited Canada brought home to North Americans the carnage of this particular war, especially in relation to civilians. At the University of Toronto on 7 July 1969, a member of the

Vietnamese women's delegation described the life of children in war-torn regions of her country:

All people must have camouflage. In some places toxic chemicals have destroyed leaves, so children going to school ... must use dry straw and things like that for camouflage. As in North Vietnam, there are air shelters in South Vietnam ... In places subjected to heavy shellings, people build their homes in tunnels ... We can't dig shelters in the lowlands, the water swamps, like the Mekong Delta, or at least we cannot dig deeply ... This is hard on women with babies; therefore women put their babies in plastic bassinettes that float in the tunnels – the water comes up to the mothers' armpits – or they hang up hammocks to put babies in and keep them dry ... The Americans have also used time-delay bombs and explosive bombs, which explode after the children come out of the shelters.[18]

Helen Boston, a member of WSP's Brooklyn chapter and a grieving mother whose son had been drafted out of high school and killed shortly after his arrival in Vietnam, attended this meeting. But first she participated in a March of Friendship. She and other members of the U.S. women's peace movement walked across the Rainbow Bridge to the middle, where they embraced the Vietnamese women who had walked partway to meet them; they then proceeded arm in arm the rest of the way until they were on Canadian soil. On the Canadian side of Niagara Falls, American, Vietnamese, and Canadian women held a meeting at which Boston spoke briefly but eloquently. Addressing her words to the Vietnamese women, she declared, "My only hope is that before my son was killed he never hurt anybody. That is what I hope."[19] The mother rage of Helen Boston and her comrades in the North American women's peace movement underscores, once more, the point made by historian Wendy Parkins that "female embodiment," in this case symbolized by a grieving mother, can be employed by "dissident citizens" to establish a critical and challenging discourse in counterpoint to an overweening and implacable discourse of war.

Thus, in the Sixties, VOW concentrated its critique of militarism and warmaking on Canadian nuclear weapons policy and on the Canadian state's complicity, through diplomatic and economic policies, in bolstering U.S. Cold War strategies, especially in Indochina. While it is not possible to gauge with any precision VOW's impact on popular political thought in this era, the organization's bold and confident public style – shrewdly posited in the consensus-building Canadian nationalist discourse that was prevalent at the time and reinforced by the non-threatening, albeit militant, iconic image of the responsible citizen-mother – helped to shape a perception among a growing number of Canadians that their nation was uniquely placed to promote peacemaking over warmaking.

The Voice of Women of Canada, the most influential Canadian peace group in the Sixties, pressed on in the following decades with its anti-war activism, and its members continued to network in creative and productive ways with women peace workers in North America and in the international arena. At the same time, VOW also sought alliances with social justice and feminist groups. As VOW's members became more deeply involved in the larger social movement culture and thought of their time, so did they evolve a deeper commitment to an enlarged understanding of what constitutes peace. For this organization, peace came to embrace issues of equity and fairness that spilled out over the boundaries of discrete movements such as civil rights and women's rights, thereby helping to change in positive ways the landscape of the social change movements of more recent times.

NOTES

1 The Halifax branch of VOW was particularly active in civil rights work. For elaboration on this aspect of VOW's history, see Frances Early, "'A Grandly Subversive Time': The Halifax Branch of the Voice of Women in the 1960s," in *Mothers of the Municipality: Women, Work, and Social Policy in Post-1945* Halifax, ed. Judith Fingard and Janet Guildford (Toronto: University of Toronto Press, 2005): 253–80.

2 For an overview discussion of Canadian women's historic progressive reform work and its persistence into the era following the Second World War, see Alison Prentice et al., *Canadian Women: A History* (Toronto: Harcourt, Brace, Jovanovich, 1988), especially 333–42. On the social reform and social democratic context for the origins of women's peace work in the United States and Canada, see Frances Early, "The Historic

Roots of the Women's Peace Movement in North America," *Canadian Woman Studies* 7, no. 4 (1986): 43–8. Insightful studies that examine the domestic ideology of the Cold War era and provide context for understanding the nature of women's peace movement protest in the Sixties in North America are Veronica Strong-Boag, "Home Dreams: Women and the Suburban Experiment in Canada, 1945–60," *Canadian Historical Review* 72 (1991): 471–504, and Elaine Tyler May, *Homeward Bound: American Families in the Cold War Era* (New York: Basic Books, 1988). Also helpful for background on the context of a resurgent women's peace movement in the United States is Dee Garrison, "'Our Skirts Gave Them Courage': The Civil Defense Protest Movement in New York City, 1955–1961," in *Not June Cleaver: Women and Gender in Postwar America, 1945–1960*, ed. Joanne Meyerowitz (Philadelphia: Temple University Press, 1994): 201–26. Garrison interprets the America of the 1950s as "an era of muffled but rising rebellion" and credits women, many of whom were middle-class housewives, with reinvigorating a "demoralized and scattered peace movement" (p. 202). A similar argument may be made in the context of Canadian women's involvement in the 1950s in such groups as the Canadian Peace Congress, provincial peace councils, the Toronto Committee for Disarmament, and the Canadian Committee for the Control of Radiation Hazards. For a study of Voice of Women – New England, an organization founded on the principles of the Canadian women's organization centred in the Boston, Mass., area, see Suzanne K. McCormack, "Good Politics Is Doing Something": Independent Diplomats and Anti-war Activists in the Vietnam-Era Peace Movement – A Collective Biography (unpublished doctoral dissertation, Boston College, 2002).

3 For an interpretation that emphasizes the role of Canadian economic elites in influencing the Canadian government to support the U.S. government's determination to defeat Vietnamese Communism at all costs, consult Victor Levant, *Quiet Complicity: Canadian Involvement in the Vietnam War* (Toronto: Between the Lines, 1986). Susan Sontag has provided an insightful exploration of the power of media representation and artistic expression of war and social violence to inspire empathy or, alternatively, to encourage indifference among citizens in Western societies. See her extended essay, *Regarding the Pain of Others* (New York: Farrar, Straus and Giroux, 2003).

4 Voice of Women papers (hereafter VOW papers), Library and Archives Canada (LAC), MG28, vol. 2, file: Sixth Annual Meeting, Reports and Agenda, 1966. The three nations appointed to membership of the Inter-

national Control Commission established to oversee that all parts of Vietnam conformed after 1954 to the Geneva Convention were Canada, India, and Poland.

5 VOW papers, LAC, MG28, vol. 2, file: Reports to Council 1965; ibid., President's Report no. 1, August 1965, file: President's Reports, 1965; ibid., Report of the VOW Delegation to Ottawa, 23 February 1965, file: Sixth Annual Meeting, Reports and Agenda, 1966.

6 See various files in VOW papers, LAC, MG28, and in the Muriel Duckworth Papers at the Public Archives of Nova Scotia (PANS) MG1, vol. 2900.

7 See the comprehensive and insightful study of WSP by Amy Swerdlow, *Women Strike for Peace: Traditional Motherhood and Radical Politics in the 1960s* (Chicago: University of Chicago Press, 1993). VOW, however, receives too little attention in this study.

8 Kay Macpherson memo, Cambridge, 9 October 1967, VOW papers, LAC, MG28, vol. 3, file: Hanoi Trip, 1968.

9 Wendy Parkins, "Protesting Like a Girl: Embodiment, Dissent, and Feminist Agency," *Feminist Theory* 1, no. 1 (2000): 59–78 (quotation on p. 73).

10 AVC pamphlet, VOW papers, LAC, MG28, vol. 6, file 8. Over time, CAVC sponsors included member of parliament Tommy Douglas, founder of Canada's Co-operative Commonwealth Federation (CCF) and first leader (1961–71) of its successor, the New Democratic Party; well-known writer Farley Mowat; René Lévesque, member of the Quebec legislature, a founder (in 1968) and then leader of the Parti Québécois, and premier of Quebec 1976–85; George Grant, the prominent "red Tory" intellectual of the Religious Studies Department at McMaster University in Hamilton, Ontario; Dennis McDermott, high-profile national labour leader, United Automobile Workers; Max Ferguson, Canadian Broadcasting Corporation commentator in Halifax, Nova Scotia, and in Toronto; established peace activist Hilary Brown of VOW British Columbia; and Rabbi A.L. Feinberg.

11 Sheila Young to Kay Macpherson, 24 November 1966, VOW papers, LAC, MG28, vol. 14, file: Knitting Project 1966–1969.

12 [Newsletter of] Ontario Voice of Women, 15 August 1967, VOW papers, LAC, MG28, vol. 14, file: Knitting Project 1966–1969.

13 VOW Papers, LAC, MG28, vol. 2, Minutes of Council Meeting, 28 January 1967; ibid., Council Meetings, Reports, 1967.

14 See Swerdlow, *Women Strike for Peace*.

15 Valida Davila to [Lil Greene], n.d., VOW papers, LAC, MG28, vol. 30, file: Projects, Project Reports.

16 Personal communication from history colleague Nancy Forestal to Frances Early, 9 May 2004. Dr Forestal specializes in Canadian women's history and is a member of the History Department at Saint Francis Xavier University in Antigonish, Nova Scotia.

17 VOW papers, LAC, MG28, passim.

18 "Voice of Women Hart House Meeting with Vietnamese Visitors," 7 July 1969, VOW papers, LAC, MG28, vol. 5, file: Vietnam, Knitting Project.

19 "Vietnamese Women Visit Canada," pamphlet dated July 1969, 3, in Muriel Duckworth Papers, PANS, MG1, vol. 2932, no. 7, "Speeches, Briefs, Reports."

4

Negotiating Citizenship:
Joyce Wieland's *Reason over Passion*

KRISTY A. HOLMES

In 1979 Margaret Trudeau published *Beyond Reason*, an autobiography that chronicles her youth through to her rather turbulent years as wife of the former prime minister of Canada, Pierre Trudeau. There is one passage I find particularly interesting:

> One day I did what in Pierre's eyes was the unforgivable. We were having a frosty argument about clothes, and suddenly I flew into the most frenzied temper. I tore off up the stairs to the landing where a Canadian quilt, designed by Joyce Weyland [sic] and lovingly embroidered in a New York loft with Pierre's motto "*La raison avant la passion*" [Reason over passion], was hanging. (Its bilingual pair was in the National Gallery.) Shaking with rage at my inability to counter his logical, reasoned arguments, I grabbed at the quilt, wrenched off the letters and hurled them down the stairs at him one by one, in an insane desire to reverse the process, to put passion before reason just this once. Pierre was icy. Vandalizing a work of art; how low could I sink? (Hildegard sewed them all on again, invisibly and without comment, the next morning.) All of it seemed beyond reason to me.[1]

Big Motion Pictures Ltd., *Trudeau: The Man, the Myth, the Movie*, 2002, film still.
Photo courtesy Kristy A. Holmes, © Big Motion Pictures Ltd.

In 2002 Big Motion Pictures produced a two-part miniseries entitled *Trudeau: The Man, the Myth, the Movie*, that features a somewhat misconstrued, albeit convincing, scene of this heated moment at the prime minister's residence. This filmic representation of Margaret literally throwing "reason" at the image of her husband on television provides a vivid example of the significance of the quilt *Reason over Passion*, made in 1968 by the Canadian artist and filmmaker Joyce Wieland (1930–1998). Trudeau may have seen this attack only as an act of vandalism on a work of art, but for Margaret the quilt signified and celebrated Trudeau's governing philosophy, and her "passionate" response suggests that she felt it was inadequate, that these two polarities should perhaps be reordered, or that reason and passion should not be polar opposites at all but, in fact, equals. To move "beyond reason," as Margaret suggests, implies that Trudeau's motto was a problematic attitude not only to bring to a marriage but also to governing.

In his speech made at the Liberal Party convention in April 1968, Trudeau uttered his now notorious phrase to an audience numbering in the thousands:

As Liberals, we rely on that most unlikely bulwark, the individual citizen, you and me, the young and the old, the famous

Joyce Wieland, *Reason over Passion*, 1968, quilted cotton, 256.5 x 302.3 x 8 cm. Collection of the National Gallery of Canada, Ottawa, © National Gallery of Canada, purchased 1970

and the unknown, the Arctic nomad and the suburbanite. It was this confidence in the individual which set me on the road which has led me to my present quest. For many years, I have been fighting for the triumph of reason over passion in politics, for the protection of the individual freedoms against the tyranny of the group, and for a just distribution of our national wealth. It was my concern with these values which led me to the Liberal party.[2]

Reason over passion premised Trudeau's Enlightenment-like valuation of reason and the classic liberal tropes of rationality, equality, and the freedom of the individual over those of passion and emotion. These were the qualities that Trudeau noted in his memoirs as those that would comprise his Just Society of the late 1960s.[3] Trudeau's concept of the individual citizen, he vehemently noted, was integral to and at the root of his liberal philosophy, and it subsequently formed the foundation of his redefinition of citizenship in Canada. In his speech, Trudeau suggested that despite age, station in life, and geographical location, everyone is essentially an individual entitled to the same freedoms and equality of opportunity. Such a utopist vision of Canada admittedly seems ideal, and it plays into the deepest myths of Canada as a peaceful, tolerant, and equal society in which identity – be it gendered, classed, or raced – is effaced in favour of good government based in a politics of rights.[4] A politics of sameness, however, during an era of unprecedented and radical demand for gender, class, and racial equality was bound to have difficulty accounting for the disparate, multiple, and collective identities that were mounting in Canada during the late 1960s and early 1970s.

In this essay, I explore how Trudeau conceptualized federalism and liberalism as the foundation of his plan for national unity and for a redefinition of citizenship in Canada during the late 1960s. In particular, I examine the federal policies Trudeau implemented over the course of the late 1960s and early 1970s that correlated with the second-wave women's movement, namely the Royal Commission on the Status of Women (RCSW). I probe how and in what ways Trudeau's plan for national unity was contingent on constructing women as individual, rights-bearing citizens and equal members of the modern Canadian nation-state. I argue that this liberalizing strategy denies the very real racial, sexual, regional, and class differences among women in Canada and that ultimately female subjectivity fundamentally questions and challenges the most basic tenets of liberal ideology and the liberal capitalist nation-state. In this sense, Trudeau's national unity project could never fully realize any woman as a citizen.

As one of Canada's most significant cultural producers of the twentieth century, Joyce Wieland was a prolific artist and filmmaker who worked in a variety of media, from painting, sculpture, and mixed media to quilting, embroidery, knitting, and film. Wieland was the first living female Canadian artist to be afforded a retrospective at both the National Gallery of Canada (1971) and the Art Gallery of Ontario (1987). Her subject matter, in both her film and non-film work, from the late 1960s to the mid-1970s is primarily concerned with national symbols, myths, and contemporaneous political issues. From 1967 to 1969, she created two quilts, *Reason over Passion* and *La raison avant la passion*, as well as an experimental film, *Reason over Passion*, which have surprisingly been afforded little critical attention in relation to their sociocultural and political contexts of production.

Wieland's artistic engagement with Trudeau – his political campaign, his philosophy of governing, his actual image – in her *Reason over Passion* works is deeply embedded in the political climate of the late Sixties in Canada and specifically in Trudeau's national unity plan and his reconceptualization of women as citizens. In the literature on Wieland, it has often been suggested that her work appears to be an apolitical celebratory engagement with the concept of the modern Canadian nation.[5] I argue, however, that her artistic involvement with a particular nexus of nationalist ideologies within a moment of developing second-wave feminism in North America is integral to understanding the ways in which, through aesthetic means, she symbolically negotiated the construction of the modern Canadian nation, contemporaneous notions of citizenship, and sexual difference. Wieland's *Reason over Passion* series uses the medium of craft and forms of filmic experimentalism in order to destabilize the masculine category of the liberal individual as the foundation for a democratic liberal welfare state. Taken as a form of cultural production, the series constitutes a radical reconsideration of the political and gendered discourses circulating in Canada at this time.

Pierre Trudeau's Canada: Liberal Hegemony or Bust

In the second volume of their polemic account of Pierre Trudeau and his political legacy, Christina McCall and Stephen Clarkson state, quite simply, "For better and for worse, Pierre Trudeau changed Canada."[6] Echoing their statement, Linda Cardinal suggests, "To be sure, it is as if the ideas of one man had been enough to transform the destiny of a whole country."[7] Writing just after Trudeau's death in 2000, Clarkson pointedly notes that even though other prime ministers have left lasting political legacies, it is Trudeau "with whom we identify the state at its apogee."[8] Even Robert and James Laxer, the left-wing political theorists and writers, note that with the election of Trudeau to power, "an era of ditch-water politics, of narrow and irrelevant inter-party bickering, was ending, opening up a new era for Canada."[9] The importance that these historians afford to the Trudeau administration (1968–79 and 1980–84) is certainly not unprecedented in Canadian historical scholarship. There are very few prime ministers in Canada's history who have remained in power as long as Trudeau and who have also so drastically and so brazenly altered the terms by which political, cultural, social, and gendered identities were formed.[10]

After becoming prime minister of Canada in 1968, Trudeau set in motion an extremely ambitious plan for national unity. At its most fundamental, this plan attempted to implement a new concept of Canadian identity that would be mobilized through constitutional reform, a redefinition of citizenship and citizen participation, and investment in "national images," in order to quell mounting collective threats (namely, Québécois nationalism) to national unity. This, in short, was Trudeau's concept of federalism, and it was deeply rooted in classic nineteenth-century liberal ideals and the belief that a strong centralist government, which recognized the rights of the individual at the federal level, would form the foundation of the modern Canadian nation.

The 1960s and early 1970s in Canada can be seen as a period of intense liberalization as Trudeau attempted to accommodate and regulate the disparate and increasingly aggressive subaltern groups within Canada by way of his federalism. As the Canadian historian Ian McKay has pointed out, liberalism is the political form of modernity in Canada,[11] and this period can be seen as a moment when this form of modernity was being challenged by previously marginalized groups, including women, the working classes, Aboriginals, and French Canadians. In this respect, it was an experiment in redefining who could be a national subject. McKay has also suggested that the process of liberalization can be seen as one of political and cultural hegemony.[12] Following the writings of Antonio Gramsci, hegemony is a concept that deals with the relationship between different classes in society and posits that for one class to exercise power over another (a governing class, for example), it must consistently coerce other classes into supporting it.[13] The dominant class does this by taking into account the interests and needs of other classes, always persuading them, and never forcing them, into support. As McKay succinctly states,

> In short, a hegemonic class exercises moral and intellectual leadership and presents itself convincingly as the "true voice of the people." At the core of hegemony is the ability of a fundamental class, through compromise and the creation of a persuasive political language, to speak to and for the "subaltern" or dominated classes it leads, and to construct a long-term historic bloc through which the rule of a few people in particular social positions comes to seem like the *only* legitimate way a society can be governed.[14]

Trudeauvian federalism, rooted in classic liberalism, was successful precisely because it was made to be hegemonic – it was constructed as the only legitimate way that Canada could remain a united country and the only way that the individual rights of all citizens, despite gender, race, class, or language, could be achieved.

Nowhere is Trudeau's federalism, liberalism, and views on nationalism and the future of Canada more pronounced than in his "Federalism, Nationalism, and Reason" (originally published in *The Future of Canadian Federalism* in 1965)[15] and "New Treason of the Intellectuals" (originally published in *Cité libre* in 1962). Although written several years before Trudeau became prime minister, these essays effectively outline his governing philosophy and serve as a blueprint for subsequent reforms to Canadian law and the reconceptualization of citizenship. In "New Treason of the Intellectuals," he envisions Canada as an experiment in a future form of federalism that could successfully govern nation-states that have multiple ethnic and linguistic groups. Trudeau states that if English and French Canada would consider collaborating to create a pluralistic state, "Canada could become the envied seat of a form of federalism that belongs to tomorrow's world. Better than the American melting-pot, Canada could offer an example to all those new Asian and African states ... who must discover how to govern their polyethnic populations with proper regard for justice and liberty ... Canadian federalism is an experiment of major proportions;

it could become a brilliant prototype for the moulding of tomorrow's civilization."[16]

Trudeau evidently had optimistic hopes for what the Canadian nation could be, and it is not surprising that as leader of the Liberal Party he conducted this experiment in ways that were rooted in classic liberalism. Trudeau's federalism saw the belief in the primacy of the rational individual, governed by reasoned political discourse, as the way to manage the nationalist passions – such as Québécois nationalism – that threatened the nation. As made evident in Trudeau's 1968 speech, the liberal concept of the individual was fundamental to his construction of citizenship in the next few years, and the policies implemented under Trudeau are reflective of his belief that a truly democratic nation-state should protect the rights and freedoms of the individual while encouraging individuals to identify with the nation rather than with regional, ethnic, classed, or gendered collectives. Trudeau's federalism is thus a precarious balance between appeasing minority groups and finding a common thread – a "compromise," or what he also calls a "national consensus"[17] – among all Canadians in order to sustain a unified nation as the ultimate will of the people.

Trudeau has often been characterized as anti-nationalist precisely because he sees such collective emotion as a threat to his centralist, federal vision of Canada. Reg Whitaker, however, has rightly argued that there is only some truth to such a claim.[18] In "New Treason of the Intellectuals," Trudeau argues that nationalism tends to be produced by the dominant ethnic group (in the case of Canada, this is white English Canadians), which establishes a nationalism based solely on the interests of the dominant group. This, of course, has obvious consequences for any minority groups that wish to identify with the nation. Trudeau states that nationalist governments are thus ultimately "intolerant, discriminatory, and, when all is said and done, totalitarian."[19] As he argues, "a truly democratic government cannot be 'nationalist,' because it must pursue the good of all its citizens, without prejudice to ethnic origin. The democratic government, then, stands for and encourages good citizenship, never nationalism."[20] Trudeau was evidently suspicious of nationalism and nationalist governments, but he was also acutely aware of how his federalism could potentially alienate certain groups within the nation. An effective government, according to Trudeau, has to find a "national consensus" between all groups. To do this, the modern nation-state cannot govern exclusively through reason alone, and it must consistently convince its citizens of its need to exist and that individual needs, regardless of gender, race, class, or language, could only be met within the framework of the nation-state. This leads Trudeau to state when nationalism is beneficial:

> It [the state] must continually persuade the generality of the people that it is in their best interest to continue as a state. And since it is physically and intellectually difficult to persuade continually through reason alone, the state is tempted to reach out for whatever emotional support it can find. Ever since history fell under the ideological shadow of the nation-state, the most convenient support has obviously been the idea of nationalism.[21]

Trudeau goes on to state how his plan for national unity, based on this type on nationalism, might work to create a national consensus, or common denominator, among all people:

> A national image must be created that will have such an appeal as to make any image of a separatist group unattractive. Resources must be diverted into such things as national flags, anthems, education, arts councils, broadcasting corporations, film boards; the territory must be bound together by a network of railways, highways, airlines; the national culture and the national economy must be protected by taxes and tariffs; ownership of resources and industry by nationals must be made a matter of policy. In short, the whole of the citizenry must be made to feel that it is only within the framework of the federal state that their language, culture, institutions, sacred traditions, and standard of living can be protected from external attack and internal strife.[22]

There is perhaps no clearer explanation than this of how liberal hegemony in Canada, from the late 1960s up to the Charter of Rights and Freedoms in 1982, unfolded historically, economically, culturally, socially, and politically. Trudeau knew that the establishment of this national consensus was key to fostering a nationalism that would establish the people of Canada as citizens of the nation rather than people with divergent racial, language, gender, and class differences. However, he was only willing to tolerate nationalism to a certain degree, and he argues that it can only exist in a balanced relationship with federalism.

The maintenance of the national consensus is difficult, as Trudeau states: "It is, of course, obvious that a national consensus will be developed in this way only if the nationalism is emotionally acceptable to all important groups within the nation ... so federalism is ultimately bound to fail if the nationalism it cultivates is unable to generate a national image which has immensely more appeal than the regional ones."[23] Trudeau ultimately sees nationalism as unable to sustain the polity, and as he polemically concludes, if a nation reaches the point of separatism, no amount of nationalism can save it: "Thus the great moment of truth arrives when it is realized that *in the last resort* the mainspring of federalism cannot be emotion but must be reason."[24] It is of no surprise that "Reason over passion" fittingly became Trudeau's motto and came to characterize his sixteen-year prime ministerial reign. While his Just Society appears to be an ideal model for an inclusive nation where all individuals are conceptualized as citizens and treated equally under federal law, such a liberalizing strategy denies the implicit inequalities that exist in liberalism itself, including, for the present discussion, the uneasy relationship between liberalism and feminism.

Negotiating Citizenship: The Second-Wave Women's Movement and Liberalism in Canada

The ways in which feminism and the second-wave women's movement played into Trudeau's national unity project is integral to understanding how women were redefined as citizens during the 1960s and early 1970s.[25] The literature on the second-wave women's movement in Canada often alludes to the close relationship it had with the Canadian state – namely, the idea that federal policy change and federal funding were characterized as the primary ways in which the demands of feminists were met. Sue Findlay has argued that

Canada, like many Western liberal democratic states in the Sixties, was searching for "solutions that would demonstrate the commitment of liberal democracies to equality without compromising their reliance on capitalism."[26] Hence, social and economic advancements towards equality for women in Canada during the late 1960s were achieved within a liberal capitalist framework that stressed participatory democracy based in a politics of rights. It thus is not surprising that the hallmark of the second-wave women's movement in Canada remains the federally sponsored Royal Commission on the Status of Women in Canada (RCSW). The impact and success of the RCSW continues to be debated, and divergent assessments have been made. Leslie Pal, for example, states that the RCSW "helped set the decade's agenda for mainstream Canadian feminism,"[27] while Ian McKay argues that "it bore the contradictory marks of an attempt to forestall feminism's more revolutionary articulation."[28] Despite debates regarding the commission's success or failure, what is important is that the RCSW and the events surrounding it reveal how equality for women in Canada during the late 1960s and early 1970s was specifically constructed within a framework of national unity and was dependent on the reconceptualization of women as rights-bearing citizens.

The RCSW was a response by the Pearson administration to the demands made by the newly formed Committee on Equality for Women (CEW) and the Fédération des femmes du Québec (FFQ) for a royal commission into the current status of women in Canada.[29] The RCSW, established in 1967 and presented to Trudeau in 1970, involved women throughout Canada who, over a period of two and a half years, came to public hearings set up in hotels, church basements, community halls, and shopping malls to voice their opinions and discuss their experiences as women.[30] As Monique Bégin, former executive secretary of the commission, notes, "the public's involvement through public hearings, briefs, and recommendations ... distinguishes royal commissions from 'expert' studies and research."[31] Bégin argues that the idea of a royal commission came largely from English Canada, and it was seen as the result of "a long-standing commitment by women's associations to reforms needed to obtain more simple justice for women, as well as a call for new social adjustments required by the buoyant 1960s."[32]

The final report, considered theoretically liberal, made 167 recommendations to the federal government, ranging from national day care to abortion reform. Scholarship on the RCSW often alludes to its symbolic rather than practical importance. Sue Findlay, for example, states that the events leading up to, and during, the establishment of the commission suggest that the Canadian state was willing to offer a formal response to women's increasing demands for equality while establishing that response as decidedly liberal.[33] Cerise Morris has argued that the importance of the RCSW was that it established for the first time that the status of women constituted a new, albeit problematic, social category that warranted treatment.[34]

In 1972 the National Action Committee on the Status of Women (NAC) was formed in order to maintain pressure on the federal government to implement the report's recommendations. The NAC, ranging in membership from the National Council of Jewish Women of Canada to the YWCA, was one of the many voluntary groups that received financial support from the federal government's Women's Program (founded in 1974), a section of the Citizenship Branch of the Department of the Secretary of State. The objective of the Women's Program was to "encourage the development of a society in which the full potential of women as citizens is recognized and utilized."[35]

Leslie Pal has persuasively argued that the global social and civil rights movements of the 1960s were addressed in Canada at the federal level by couching equality – for women, ethnic minorities, and French Canadians – in terms of national unity and citizen participation.[36] Pal examined the Citizenship Branch of the Department of the Secretary of State in order to explore the ways in which this branch of the federal government funded, among other things, voluntary women's groups such as the NAC through the Women's Program. The programs were designed and funded to encourage active citizen participation in voluntary organizations that were meant to alleviate feelings of social injustice.[37] Pal notes that this branch underwent massive restructuring under Trudeau and that while national unity through citizen participation became the primary mandate of the branch, this was also dependent on "a redefinition of the meaning of citizenship and a new articulation of the proper role and relationship of government to voluntary organizations."[38] Pal suggests that it may seem paradoxical that the state appeared to fund the very organizations that threatened its unity, but she argues that active citizen participation was seen "to foster greater allegiance to national institutions through a feeling that those institutions were open to popular forces."[39] Pal's examination of the Citizenship Branch under Trudeau makes it clear that participatory democracy and the funding of women's groups were integral to constructing women as citizens in order to cultivate a sense of national unity.

Historians Jill Vickers and Micheline de Sève have built on Pal's suggestion that under Trudeau women were constructed as active citizens in the developing modern Canadian nation. While the nation, nationalism, and nation building, as products of modernity, have characteristically been seen as structures and processes that have treated women unequally,[40] Vickers and de Sève argue that "aspects of Canada as a 'New World' society provide a greater opportunity for some women, especially majority-culture women, to participate actively in nation building and to combine nationalist and feminist aspirations."[41] Vickers explores this idea further, arguing that at various times throughout the twentieth century, including the late 1960s and early 1970s, white English Canadian women enjoyed a positive relationship with nationalism and the nation-building project.[42] Vickers suggests that under the guise of civic nationalism the "federal Liberals attempted to co-opt the women's movement into their Canadian national-unity project by funding many women's organizations, mainly because they hoped undifferentiated 'feminism' would cut across the cleavage of Québec nationalism."[43] By funding women's groups and implementing policies from RCSW, it was hoped that both English and French Canadian women would see the attainment of gender-based equality as equivalent to biculturalism and multiculturalism. In this sense, under Trudeau, in order to quell mounting threats to national unity, the liberal individual was recast and the national unity project took on a gendered dimension that sought to have all women identify their equality within the framework of the nation by entrenching gender rights in law at the federal level.

Vickers's argument is certainly persuasive, and there is no doubt that women in Trudeau's Canada had begun to be envisaged as citizens entitled to basic fundamental rights and equality of opportunity.

Trudeau's desire to have women identify their equality within the framework of the nation-state supposes that all women – regardless of race, class, language, and regional differences – could be reconceptualized as individuals with the same rights and freedoms as men and have equal access to the means of production; hence, they could in theory be citizens. While this classic conceptualization of a democratic liberal state appears to be conducive to the feminist politics of the 1960s and early 1970s, recognizing women as individuals and extending to them the individual rights and freedoms that establish them as citizens in a civil society presents a far more complex issue.

Recent critical feminist discussions of liberalism point out that while the liberal demand for equal rights has always been characteristic of feminism, the universalizing tendencies of liberalism that erase such identity markers as class and race pose a paradoxical challenge to feminist-liberalism itself. Anne Phillips, a feminist critic of liberal theory, argues that by "insisting on equality as something we claim *despite* all differences, women have been encouraged to deny aspects of themselves and to conform to some unitary norm," and second, "this norm was never gender-neutral."[44] Like many feminist critics of liberal theory and liberalism, Phillips points out this paradox in liberalism and liberal-feminism: that while individual rights appear conducive to women's equality, universalizing the subject poses the danger of erasing difference. Phillips also rightly points out that while the individual is an abstract category, it is also a patriarchal construct.

One of the most critical attacks on the liberal individual and liberalism in general can be found in the work of Carole Pateman. In her seminal text, *The Sexual Contract*, she argues that liberalism fundamentally denies women the ability to participate fully in civil society because the category "individual" is patriarchal and can never be occupied by women: "The denial of civil equality to women means that the feminist aspiration must be to win acknowledgement for women as 'individuals.' Such an aspiration can never be fulfilled. The 'individual' is a patriarchal category. The individual is masculine and his sexuality is understood accordingly."[45] Pateman argues that the shaping of the individual in liberal theory as masculine has devastating consequences for conceptualizing women as citizens because, essentially, they never can be. As she states, "There is no set of clothes available for a citizen who is a woman, no vision available within political theory of the new democratic woman ... All that is clear is that if women are to be citizens as *women*, as autonomous, equal, yet sexually different beings from men, democratic theory and practice has to undergo a radical transformation."[46]

While Pateman's arguments are exceedingly more complex than can be dealt with here, the fundamental point is that women's involvement as citizens in the public realm is historically, and currently, problematic because women have been constructed as intimately bound to the private or domestic realm. These two spheres are not separate; they are mutually dependent on the division of labour and on prescribed social and political roles that each possesses. As Pateman argues, when women are conceptualized as citizens, there is no "vision" for understanding how they can occupy this position in civil society.[47] It is this critical stance on women as citizens that Joyce Wieland explored through aesthetic means in her *Reason over Passion* series.

Joyce Wieland's *Reason over Passion*

In the autumn of 1962, Joyce Wieland and her then-husband, artist and filmmaker Michael Snow, left Toronto and moved into a run-down loft in New York City's Greenwich Village. They had left Canada to find the "real" art scene. As Wieland recounts, "Mike and I were making a lot of trips there ... He just felt that's where he should be, and I certainly felt that what was going on there was incredible – things were really happening."[48] But Wieland enjoyed little success in New York and exhibited, with few exceptions, only in Toronto and primarily at her dealer Avrom Isaacs's gallery. She has attributed this largely to the difficulty she faced as a woman trying to compete within the male-dominated artistic arena of New York City in the Sixties: "I felt that there was something inferior – as many, many women artists will say – or missing in me so that I could never be taken seriously or equally. I felt that they were together, all the men, and I could be a part only by being this eccentric or nice little person or something like that."[49] While Wieland was living in New York, her aesthetic shifted from large painted canvases to smaller paintings, three-dimensional objects, and mixed media that demonstrated an increased concern with her surroundings: the Vietnam War, racism, popular culture, ecology, disaster, and sexuality. By the late 1960s, however, there was a marked shift in Wieland's aesthetic and subject matter as she became involved in the experimental avant-garde film movement in New York City as well as in issues of Canadian nationalism, politics, and feminism. The result of this shift is exemplified in Wieland's 1968 *Reason over Passion* quilts and her 1969 film *Reason over Passion*.

On 4 April 1968, Wieland boarded a plane to Ottawa to attend the Liberal Party convention at the Civic Centre. It was here that Trudeau claimed victory as the new leader of the Liberal Party. On the way back from the convention Wieland noted, "My friend Mary [Mitchell] and I had been reading about Trudeau; the *New York Times*, the Canadian papers, everybody was talking about him ... Yes I got the idea for the quilts and what the film would be on the way back reading Trudeau being quoted in the paper: 'Reason over passion, that is the theme of all my writings.'"[50]

It is hardly surprising that Wieland made the journey to Ottawa that spring, since she, along with Mary Mitchell and others, had formed a support group in New York City for Trudeau's leadership, called Canadians Abroad for Trudeau.[51] On 21 May 1968 she hosted a "quilt-in" at her New York loft and invited female Canadian expatriates to help sew a quilt as a gift for Trudeau. That quilt was *La raison avant la passion*, and its English-language counterpart, made subsequently, was purchased by the National Gallery of Canada in 1970. Both quilts are massive brightly coloured works, scattered with stuffed hearts and large letters spelling out Trudeau's political philosophy. As a newspaper column reported shortly afterwards, "An event billed as the world's first political quilt-in was held last evening in the third-floor walkup apartment-art studio of Mr. and Mrs. Michael Snow in Lower Manhattan. Canadian-born women, and even one or two men among the hundred or so persons present, sewed busily on an art quilt which will be sent to Canada's bachelor Prime Minister."[52]

On 8 November 1969, Wieland and Snow hosted a large party at their loft, attended by Canadian expatriates and various New York artists and writers, as well as the guest of honour – Pierre Trudeau.[53] Afterwards, Trudeau sent Wieland and Snow a letter thanking them

Joyce Wieland, *La raison avant la passion*, 1968, quilted cotton, 244.7 x 305.5 x 8 cm. Estate of Pierre Elliott Trudeau, Montreal, © National Gallery of Canada

for the party, adding, "Thank you as well for the magnificent quilt which, if I estimate correctly, must have taken almost as much work as the organization of the party. It is a very sensitive and thoughtful gift and I am honoured to receive it."[54] In his own handwriting Trudeau concluded, "and in the hope of seeing you again, with some films!"[55]

By 1969, Wieland had completed fourteen experimental films and had become deeply involved in the underground avant-garde film scene in New York City.[56] The film *Reason over Passion* was recorded between 1967 and 1968, and was completed in 1969 and premiered at the National Arts Centre in Ottawa. The film is a cross-Canada journey recorded almost entirely through the windows of a train and a car. It begins in Cape Breton Island in the spring, with the waves of the Atlantic Ocean, and ends in the snow-capped Rocky Mountains just short of the Pacific Ocean. Where Ontario should be, the journey is interrupted by a recording of an elementary school French lesson,

sroeevor ssiapon

Joyce Wieland, *Reason over Passion*, 1967–69, film still. Photo courtesy of the Film Reference Library, Toronto, © Cinémathèque québécoise

followed by fifteen minutes of grainy footage of Trudeau, filmed by Wieland at the 1968 Liberal convention. Throughout the film, 537 permutations of "reason over passion" flash across the bottom of the screen and are interspersed with an artificial beeping sound. At the beginning of the film, the Canadian flag flashes intermittently on the screen, along with the words of *O Canada*, a close-up shot of Wieland's lips silently mouthing the words, and shots of Trudeau's phrase, "La Raison Avant la Passion ... c'est le theme de tous mes écrits" and "About Reason over Passion that's the theme of all my writings."

Reason over Passion is a long film, eighty minutes in duration, and it is incredibly boring in parts – but boring in a deliberate way. Viewers become acutely aware of the film's length as the seemingly endless sequences of vast, empty stretches of land echo the feeling one might have on completing the cross-Canada journey oneself. While the narrative of the journey is important, it is not at the expense of the film's modernist structural character. Avant-garde structural film concerned

Joyce Wieland, *Reason over Passion*, 1967–69, film still. Photo courtesy of Kristy A. Holmes, © Cinémathèque québécoise

itself with filmic effects and the manipulation of the celluloid and narrative structure.[57] This undermined the modern tradition of film-making by subverting the content or story in favour of process and textuality. In *Reason over Passion*, Wieland's manipulation of the film's textuality is evident in the way she distorts and blurs certain images: for instance, the footage of Trudeau; her use of sound and text as symbolic signifiers of technology and rationality; and the juxtaposition of "real" footage and computer-generated footage. Wieland used these structural techniques not only to rework filmic representation but also to subvert traditional pictorial representations of the Canadian landscape by artists such as the Group of Seven, while simultaneously recalling and manipulating the traditional nationalistic associations such depictions evoke.

Wieland's turn to the subject matter of the nation, and especially to Trudeau, in the late 1960s has always seemed to me to be particularly unusual. As previously discussed, several feminist scholars have noted how the nation and nationalism have consistently been at odds with feminist politics. Whereas Jill Vickers suggested that under Trudeau the relationship between majority-culture women and the nation-building project was positive, Anne Phillips and Carole Pateman suggested that liberalism was fundamentally unable to construct women as individuals and thus as equal citizens. The fact that Trudeau incorporated women into his national unity plan and that the federal government deemed the status of women to be an issue warranting a royal commission may explain why Wieland turned to the subject matter of the nation and famously proclaimed, "I think of Canada as female."[58] Her *Reason over Passion* series suggests, however, that Trudeau's reasoned federalism was unable to fully realize women as citizens. Wieland's series negotiates contemporaneous constructions of citizenship and second-wave feminism, which results in an alternative version of the nation – what we might call the gendered nation.

Wieland's relationship with Trudeau, personally and aesthetically, is a particularly odd one, especially as her apparent fascination with Trudeau was ambivalent. Although Wieland evidently supported Trudeau in his leadership, by the early 1970s she was increasingly critical of his political project. For example, in undated notes, which appear to have been made to accompany a screening of the film *Reason over Passion*, Wieland wrote:

> Then came the fantasies of being a government propagandist. When you are editing a film for three months you may have fantasies. 12 hrs. a day. I thought I was Lennie Riefenstahl. It was due perhaps to editing Trudeau ... would he be a good leader? Or just a politician? Irony came wandering in ... in the form of applause (in the introduction) for his statement "reason over passion ... that is the theme of all my writing" ... French lesson is a direct reference to Trudeau's idea of bilingualism ... we must all speak French so that the French Canadian will feel at home in his own country (I like the idea) ... The film is sewn together with flags 10 different kinds.[59]

Wieland's ambivalence is evident here; she questions Trudeau's effectiveness as a leader, but also positions herself as a "government propagandist," supporting such classic Trudeauvian reforms as bilingualism, which is reiterated in her literal and symbolic use of French and

English in her *Reason over Passion* quilts. In several interviews from the early 1970s to the mid-1980s, Wieland consistently discussed her belief in her role as propagandist. In unpublished parts of an interview with Pierre Théberge, the curator of contemporary Canadian art at the National Gallery of Canada, Wieland stated that she imagined she was working for the government when she made *Reason over Passion* and felt that at the time Trudeau was "an interesting man ... and maybe a creative man."[60] In a 1971 interview with Wieland, Kay Armatage asked about her use of Trudeau in *Reason over Passion*: "Do you think of it as a process of objectification of Trudeau, in the way that women have always been objectified in movies?" To which Wieland responded, "No, I guess what I'm doing to Trudeau is putting him on for his statement 'Reason over passion – that is the theme of all my writings.' Taking the words Reason over Passion in the beginning of the film, treating them as a propaganda slogan, and through permutation, turning them into visual poetry, into a new language."[61]

In 1986 Barbara Stevenson asked Wieland, "I'm wondering about your attitude about Trudeau ... what message about Trudeau were you conveying in those works?" To which Wieland replied, "I was just saying that he had this reason above everything. And it really should be reason *and* passion in a person. But this man is only reason over passion, and ultimately, he's a psychopath." Stevenson: "You'd go that far?" Wieland: "Oh, yes."[62] Wieland went on to tell Stevenson that her support of Trudeau waned after he implemented the War Measures Act: "What do you do after that when you find out that the person's heart is closed and that the War Measures Act could take place?"[63] In an undated interview with Joyce Wieland the interviewer, identified as AL (most likely Ardele Lister), asked, "What influenced you to make work about Canada?" Wieland responded:

I didn't fit in there [New York] ... I was engaged in a lot of reading about Canada at that time, and a lot of people here were writing things that were very important. Some of the really interesting writing on economics and independence and stuff were being written at that time. That made me think that there should be an artistic response to this kind of new philosophy, this new thinking in nationalism. I got interested in propaganda, about the Trudeau campaign and so on that I conceived the idea ... of the quilts and the film combined, *Reason Over Passion*. To me those aren't really political films, but it was like tasting the idea of responding to the culture, or even having dialogue with the political body, as it were, of the country.[64]

This statement suggests that Wieland felt a sense of obligation to respond artistically to her environment which, despite living in New York City from 1962 to 1971, she identified as the contemporary political and cultural milieu of Canada. In each of these statements Wieland noted the importance of Trudeau and his national unity project to her work, and even though she had supported his political campaign, her *Reason over Passion* works suggest anything but a straightforward sign of support. The quilts and the film draw from existing propaganda and use craft and filmic experimentalism as a new form of feminist propaganda, which critiques and destabilizes the patriarchal construction of the individual as the foundation of the modern capitalist liberal nation-state. Such an act shifts embedded notions of what propaganda traditionally implies and contaminates its usefulness as a reasoned, political discourse.

Wieland as a feminist propagandist acts as a translator of her environment. The two *Reason over Passion* quilts and the film interfere in the realm of the *techne*. Reason, rationality, and technology are reclaimed, reordered, and hence regendered by Wieland as she insists on the transparency of her authorship. She does this through the aesthetic of craft, which has traditional associations with the feminine domestic realm. Trudeau's motto rendered in the quilted medium humorously suggests the absurdity of reason being the primary ideological factor behind the modern Canadian nation. The production of the quilts by a group of women works in a similar way by dislocating the masculine modernist tradition of authorial power in favour of a collective effort by women. Wieland makes her authorship evident in the film in such scenes as that in which the words of *O Canada* immediately cut away to a close-up of her lips silently mouthing them, making the viewer aware – in no uncertain terms – who the author of this film is. The image of the words of *O Canada* directly cutting to Wieland mouthing them positions Wieland as a national subject, dutifully singing the national anthem, while simultaneously suggesting that it is only through her own image, which focuses on lips – a highly sexualized signifier of "woman" – that her version of the nation can be articulated. This firmly establishes Wieland as author of this alternative gendered discourse of nation, literally claiming and "representing" her own version of the anthem as intimately bound to the bodily rather than rational word.

Just as "reason over passion" has been regendered by way of the quilted medium so too have the same words in the film by way of their reordering into nonsensical words: the *techne* of language is rendered useless and void of the knowledge and power it once signified. Wieland's depiction of Trudeau in the film again reiterates ambivalence. Her experimentation with the image of Trudeau by reshooting the original footage from the Liberal convention allows her to use different lenses, tint the celluloid, and play with the camera speed, focus, and iris, which results in a distorted and obviously manipulated image of the prime minister, reinforcing its representational nature. The real image of Trudeau is again only an illusion, and the viewer can access him – really an image – only through Wieland's distortions. Wieland's engagement with the *techne* of language and political culture, combined with her manipulation of signifiers of the nation, such as the land and Trudeau, use artistic means as a form of citizenship practice, positioning herself and her artistic production in both feminist and nationalist terms.

In February 2005 the National Gallery of Canada held its blockbuster exhibition, *The Sixties in Canada*. It featured, for the first time since their debut at Wieland's retrospective in 1971, both of the *Reason over Passion* quilts. When I first saw *La raison avant la passion*, all I could think of was Margaret ripping the letters off and throwing them at Trudeau – at her anger towards reason over passion – and the similar frustration that Wieland felt towards such a rigid and dichotomous governing philosophy. Situating Wieland as a cultural producer and examining her personal and artistic relationship with Trudeau's national unity project, his federalism, liberalism, and political campaign, suggest the ways in which white English Canadian women were envisaged as part of the shifting definition of citizenship in Canada in the late 1960s and early 1970s, and also the limits that such a construction entails. Wieland's vehement identification with the nation was not that of the liberal civic nationalism with which she has often been associated, but rather one that questions the limitations inherent in such discourse. Wieland's *Reason over Passion* quilts and film rework Trudeau's governing philosophy and question the inherent liberal values of reason and rationality as those that could comprise new definitions of citizenship and identity for women in Canada. Like Margaret Trudeau, Wieland suggests in her *Reason over Passion* series that to go "beyond reason" is an integral step towards a truly Just Society.

NOTES

1 Margaret Trudeau, *Beyond Reason* (New York: Paddington Press, 1979), 240–1.

2 Pierre Elliott Trudeau, "Transcript of Remarks of the Honourable Pierre E. Trudeau at the Liberal Leadership Convention, 5 April 1968," quoted in *The Sixties in Canada*, Denise Leclerc and Pierre Dessureault (Ottawa: National Gallery of Canada/Canadian Museum of Contemporary Photography, 2005), 43–6.

3 Pierre Trudeau, *Memoirs* (Toronto: McClelland & Stewart, 1993), 87–8. See also Pierre Trudeau and Thomas S. Axworthy, "The Values of a Just Society," in *Towards a Just Society: The Trudeau Years*, ed. Trudeau and Axworthy, 357–85 (Markham: Viking/Penguin Books, 1990).

4 A critical discussion of these myth complexes can be found in Eva MacKey, *The House of Difference: Cultural Politics and National Identity in Canada* (Toronto: University of Toronto Press, 2002), and Daniel Francis, *National Dreams: Myth, Memory, and Canadian History* (Vancouver: Arsenal Pulp Press, 1997).

5 See, for example, Dennis Reid, *A Concise History of Canadian Painting*, 2nd edn. (Toronto: Oxford University Press, 1988); David Burnett and Marilyn Schiff, *Contemporary Canadian Art* (Edmonton: Hurtig, 1983); and Barry Lord, *The History of Painting in Canada: Toward a People's Art* (Toronto: NC Press, 1974).

6 Christina McCall and Stephen Clarkson, *Trudeau and Our Times: The Heroic Delusion*, vol. 2 (Toronto: McClelland & Stewart, 1994), 12.

7 Linda Cardinal, "Citizenship Politics in Canada and the Legacy of Pierre Elliott Trudeau," in *From Subjects to Citizens: A Hundred Years of*

Citizenship in Australia and Canada, ed. Pierre Boyer, Linda Cardinal, and David Headon (Ottawa: University of Ottawa Press, 2004), 163.

8 Stephen Clarkson, "Charisma and Contradiction: The Legacy of Pierre Elliott Trudeau," *Queen's Quarterly* 107, no. 4 (2000): 605.

9 James Laxer and Robert Laxer, "The Canadian Liberal System: Trudeau's Inheritance," in *The Liberal Idea of Canada: Pierre Trudeau and the Question of Canada's Survival* (Toronto: Lorimer, 1977), 15.

10 For general discussions of the early Trudeau administration see Christina McCall-Newman, "Pierre Trudeau and the Politics of Passion: The Liberal Party, 1965–1972," in *Grits: An Intimate Portrait of the Liberal Party*, 53–134 (Toronto: Macmillan, 1982), and Christina McCall and Stephen Clarkson, *Trudeau and Our Times: The Magnificent Obsession*, vol. 1 (Toronto: McClelland & Stewart, 1990).

11 Ian McKay, *The Challenge of Modernity: A Reader on Post-Confederation Canada* (Toronto: McGraw-Hill Ryerson, 1992), xi.

12 Ibid., xiv.

13 For a succinct discussion of Gramsci's concept of hegemony see Roger Simon, "Gramsci's Concept of Hegemony," in *Gramsci's Political Thought: An Introduction* (London: Lawrence & Wishart, 1991), 22–9.

14 McKay, *The Challenge of Modernity*, xv.

15 See P.A. Crepeau and C.B. Macpherson, eds., *The Future of Canadian Federalism* (Toronto: University of Toronto Press, 1965).

16 Pierre Trudeau, "New Treason of the Intellectuals," in *Federalism and the French Canadians* (Toronto: Macmillan, 1968), 178–9.

17 Ibid., 189 and 193.

18 Reg Whitaker, "Reason, Passion, and Interest: Pierre Trudeau's Eternal Liberal Triangle," in *A Sovereign Idea: Essays on Canada as a Democratic Community* (Montreal & Kingston: McGill-Queen's University Press, 1992), 153.

19 Trudeau, "New Treason of the Intellectuals," 169.

20 Ibid.

21 Trudeau, "Federalism, Nationalism, and Reason," in *Federalism and the French Canadians*, 189.

22 Ibid., 193.

23 Ibid.

24 Ibid., 194.

25 It is beyond the scope of this chapter to provide a nuanced discussion of the development of second-wave feminism in Canada. For such discussions, see Cerise Morris, "'Determination and Thoroughness': The Movement for a Royal Commission on the Status of Women in

Canada," *Atlantis* 5, no. 2 (1980): 1–21; Ruth Roach Pierson, Marjorie Griffin Cohen, Paula Bourne, and Philinda Masters, eds., *Canadian Women's Issues: Strong Voices*, vol. 1 (Toronto: Lorimer, 1993); Constance Backhouse and David H. Flaherty, eds., *Challenging Times: The Women's Movement in Canada and the United States* (Montreal & Kingston: McGill-Queen's University Press, 1992); Roberta Hamilton, *Gendering the Vertical Mosaic: Feminist Perspectives on Canadian Society* (Mississauga: Copp Clark, 1996); Judy Rebick, *Ten Thousand Roses: The Making of a Feminist Revolution* (Toronto: Penguin, 2005); The Clio Collective, *Quebec Women: A History* (Toronto: Clio, 1987); and Sandra Burt, "Women's Issues and the Women's Movement in Canada since 1970," in *The Politics of Gender, Ethnicity, and Language in Canada*, ed., Alan Cairns and Cynthia Williams, 111–69 (Toronto: University of Toronto Press, 1986).

26 Sue Findlay, "Facing the State: The Politics of the Women's Movement Reconsidered," in *Feminism and Political Economy: Women's Work, Women's Struggles*, ed. Heather Jon Maroney and Meg Luxton (Toronto: Methuen, 1987), 34.

27 Leslie A. Pal, *Interests of State: The Politics of Language, Multiculturalism, and Feminism in Canada* (Montreal & Kingston: McGill-Queen's University Press), 113.

28 Ian McKay, *Rebels, Reds, Radicals: Rethinking Canada's Left History* (Toronto: Between the Lines, 2005), 199.

29 The Committee on Equality for Women, founded in 1966, was led by Laura Sabia and was an amalgam of thirty-two women's organizations. The Fédération des femmes du Québec was founded in 1966 by Thérèse Casgrain (who had also founded the Quebec chapter of the women's peace group, Voice of Women) and Monique Bégin. See Pal, *Interests of State*, 113.

30 For an excellent discussion of the social history of the RCSW, see Jane Arscott, "Twenty-Five Years and Sixty-Five Minutes after the Royal Commission on the Status of Women," *International Journal of Canadian Studies* 11 (Spring 1995): 33–56.

31 Monique Bégin, "The Royal Commission on the Status of Women in Canada: Twenty Years Later," in *Challenging Times*, ed. Backhouse and Flaherty, 33.

32 Ibid., 24.

33 Findlay, "Facing the State," 31.

34 Morris, "'Determination and Thoroughness,'" 1.

35 Pal, *Interests of State*, 216.

36 Ibid., 251.

37 Ibid., 109.

38 Ibid., 105.

39 Ibid., 251.

40 Recent critical discussions by feminist theorists argue that nationalism is a process that has traditionally constructed women as unequal members of the state and that nationalism itself is a gendered phenomenon. See Himani Bannerji, *The Dark Side of the Nation: Essays on Multiculturalism, Nationalism, and Gender* (Toronto: Canadian Scholars Press, 2000); Anthony Smith, *Nationalism and Modernism: A Critical Survey of Recent Theories of Nations and Nationalism* (London & New York: Routledge, 1998); Veronica Strong-Boag, Sherrill Grace, Avigail Eisenberg and Joan Anderson, eds., *Painting the Maple: Essays on Race, Gender, and the Construction of Canada* (Vancouver: UBC Press, 1998); Sylvia Walby, "Women and Nation," *International Journal of Comparative Sociology* 33, no. 1–2 (1992); Lois West, ed., *Feminist Nationalism* (New York: Routledge, 1997); Nira Yuval-Davis and Floya Anthias, eds., *Woman-Nation-State* (London: Sage, 1989); Nira Yuval-Davis, *Gender and Nation* (London: Sage, 1997).

41 Jill Vickers and Micheline de Sève, "Introduction," *Journal of Canadian Studies* 35, no. 2 (2000): 7.

42 Jill Vickers, "Feminisms and Nationalisms in English Canada," *Journal of Canadian Studies* 35, no. 2 (2000): 132.

43 Ibid., 138.

44 Anne Phillips, "Universal Pretensions in Political Thought," in *Democracy and Difference* (Cambridge: Polity Press, 1993), 56.

45 Carole Pateman, "Feminism and the Marriage Contract," in *The Sexual Contract* (Stanford: Stanford University Press, 1988), 184–5.

46 Carole Pateman, *The Disorder of Women: Democracy, Feminism, and Political Theory* (Cambridge: Polity Press, 1989), 14.

47 See Pateman's chapter, "Feminist Critiques of the Public/Private Dichotomy," in *The Disorder of Women*, 118–40.

48 Lauren Rabinovitz, "An Interview with Joyce Wieland," *Afterimage* (May 1981): 8.

49 Ibid., 11.

50 Ibid., 10.

51 See David Stein, "Trudeau's Got Friends in New York," *Toronto Daily Star*, undated, Joyce Wieland fonds, the Clara Thomas Archives and Special Collections, York University (hereafter JW, CTA), 2001-058/003, file 8.

52 "Political Quilt-in Held by N.Y. Trudeau Fans," undated and unauthored newspaper clipping, JW, CTA, 1991-014/VIII, file 73.

53 Stan Fischler, "Pierre's the Star of an Arty Party in New York Loft," *Toronto Daily Star*, 11 November 1969, JW, CTA, 1992-018/003, file 42.

54 JW, CTA, 1992-018/003, file 42.

55 Ibid.

56 For a discussion of Wieland's work in film, see Kathryn Elder, ed., *The Films of Joyce Wieland* (Waterloo: Wilfrid Laurier Press, 1999). For a discussion of women avant-garde filmmakers in New York City, see Lauren Rabinovitz, *Points of Resistance: Women, Power, and Politics in the New York Avant-garde Cinema, 1943–71*, 2nd edn. (Urbana & Chicago: University of Illinois Press, 2003).

57 For a description of avant-garde structural film, see P. Adams Sitney, "Structural Film," in *Film Culture: An Anthology*, ed. P. Adams Sitney, 326–48 (London: Secker and Warburg, 1971).

58 Kay Armatage, "Kay Armatage Interviews Joyce Wieland," *Take One* 3, no. 2 (1970, published 1972): 24.

59 JW, CTA, 1993-009/010, file 120.

60 *True Patriot Love/Véritable amour patriotique* exhibition files, National Gallery of Canada fonds, National Gallery of Canada Archives, 32.

61 Armatage, "Kay Armatage Interviews Joyce Wieland," 25.

62 JW, CTA, 1999-003/005, file 05.

63 Ibid.

64 JW, CTA, 1991-014/005, file 73.

FURTHER READING

Cairns, Alan, and Cynthia Williams. *Constitutionalism, Citizenship and Society in Canada*. Vol. 33. Toronto: University of Toronto Press in cooperation with the Royal Commission on the Economic Union and Development Prospects for Canada, 1985

– *The Politics of Gender, Ethnicity, and Language in Canada*. Vol. 34. Toronto: University of Toronto Press in cooperation with the Royal Commission on the Economic Union and Development Prospects for Canada, 1986

Conley, Christine. "*True Patriot Love*: Joyce Wieland's Canada." In *Art, Nation, and Gender: Ethnic Landscapes, Myths, and Mother-Figures*, ed. Tricia Cusack and Sìghle Bhreathnach-Lynch, 95–112. Burlington, Vt: Ashgate, 2003

Dietz, Mary. "Context Is All: Feminism and Theories of Citizenship." In *Dimensions of Radical Democracy: Pluralism, Citizenship, Community*, ed. Chantal Mouffe. London & New York: Verso, 1992

Eisenstein, Zillah R. *The Radical Future of Liberal Feminism*. Boston: Northeastern University Press, 1986

Findlay, Sue. "Feminist Struggles with the Canadian State: 1966–1988." RFR/DRF, *Resources for Feminist Research* 17, no. 3 (1988): 5–9

Fleming, Marie. *Joyce Wieland*. Toronto: Art Gallery of Ontario/Key Porter Books, 1987

Longfellow, Brenda. "Gendering the Nation: Symbolic Stations in Canadian and Quebec Film History." In *Ghosts in the Machine: Women and Cultural Policy in Canada and Australia*, ed. Alison Beale and Annette Van Den Bosch, 163–80. Toronto: Garamond Press, 1998

McRoberts, Kenneth. *Misconceiving Canada: The Struggle for National Unity*. Toronto: Oxford University Press, 1997

Phillips, Anne. *Engendering Democracy*. Cambridge: Polity Press, 1991

– ed. *Feminism and Equality*. Oxford: Blackwell, 1987

Rabinovitz, Lauren. "The Development of Feminist Strategies in the Experimental Films of Joyce Wieland." *Film Reader* 5 (1982): 132–40

Sloan, Johanne. "Joyce Wieland at the Border: Nationalism, the New Left, and the Question of Political Art in Canada." *Journal of Canadian Art History* 26, (2005): 81–104

5

A Crash Course in Manhood:
Men, Cars, and Risk in Postwar Vancouver

CHRISTOPHER DUMMITT

At their 1960 annual meeting, members of the Vancouver Traffic and Safety Council listened to an impassioned keynote speech by W.A. Bryce, executive director of the Canadian Highway Safety Council. Bryce told the audience of local notables something they often told themselves: that the world was a dangerous place and the danger they faced was new. "Life in the world today is not the casual easygoing existence that our grandfathers knew one hundred years ago or even fifty years ago," he claimed. "Yes, life today – on the streets or in the skies – does not guarantee that we shall all die in our beds." The modern age had given birth to the threat of the traffic crash and nuclear war; such dangers were the progeny of modern technological life. In both cases, Bryce warned, one could easily become "baffled and frustrated" by the apparent dearth of solutions. Yet he decried such fatalism. Although modern technologies created many problems, they also offered solutions. He admitted to having no immediate solution to the atomic threat but claimed, "Highway accidents ... are a different matter. They are within our experience – we do know their cause and we can provide their cure."[1]

What was Bryce's cure? How did he hope to eradicate the harm caused by the automobile age? If attendees at the annual meeting wanted a novel approach, they were surely disappointed. For Bryce's solutions mirrored what local traffic safety advocates had been arguing since the early years of the automobile. He called for a smattering of different programs, from more education to better enforcement, all of which fitted neatly into the range of accepted traffic safety discourse. Safety experts, Bryce included, held that individual drivers caused accidents and that the best way to stop accidents was to find better ways of encouraging self-discipline. This approach reflected a technologically deterministic view of modern life, which assumed that humans, not technology, needed to change.

What made Bryce's speech memorable (and the reason we are dwelling on it here) was the way he grasped for the profound in his final words. Wrapping up his speech, he quoted (selectively) from Rudyard Kipling's poem of paternal advice, "If":

> If you can keep your head when all about you
> Are losing theirs and blaming it on you,
> If you can wait and not be tired by waiting,
> If you can fill the unforgiving minute
> With sixty seconds' worth of run,
> Yours is the Earth and everything that's in it
> And – what is more – you'll be a man, my son!

At the end of the poem, Bryce added a line of his own, rewording the message of manhood achieved so that it matched the requirements of the automobile age. "And what is more," he claimed, "you'll be a good driver, a good insurance risk, with a low insurance premium and a long life expectation."[2] It may not have been smashing poetry, but Bryce's addition is a telling pronouncement on the connection between traffic accidents, risk, and masculinity in the postwar years. Bryce called on traffic experts to create safe drivers as the best way of eliminating traffic accidents. And how did one make good drivers? The answer was simple: you turned them into good men.

My essay is a cultural history of exactly this connection between driving and masculinity in one of Canada's fastest growing and most important postwar cities, Vancouver. Gender historians of the postwar years have been keen to examine men in their role as fathers and breadwinners. We now know a good deal about the domestic politics of suburban life and about the way ideals of male breadwinning pervaded social and political life.[3] There were, however, other important ways in which postwar Canadians thought about being a man. One of the most significant was the connection made between being manly and being modern – the link in popular discourse between technocratic and expert modernity and the norms of masculinity. And nowhere is this clearer than in the language used to talk about automobiles, and especially traffic safety.

In the years before the Sixties, ideals of the good driver and the good man, ostensibly separate, shared many characteristics. Their point of convergence was their shared support for a disciplined type of character, one that stressed diligent awareness and foresight as the epitome of responsible behaviour. This reasonable and responsible man ideal is long-standing, and one of the ways it has continued to exert such force is by continually being rewritten into new codes of behaviour. Earlier in the century, it was more likely to be uttered along with moralistic calls for good character and self-restraint,[4] but in the 1940s and 1950s it fitted itself into the language of technocratic risk management. In those years, a group of experts assumed that the traits of the ideal middle-class male were also the traits of the ideal driver, and they mapped one set of characteristics onto the other. In this way, a set of instructions, which allegedly applied to both sexes equally, in fact became imbued with a gender ideology that saw good driving as a kind of masculine achievement. The safety experts updated the reasonable man ideal. To the extent that knowing how to handle a car was an important and privileged type of knowledge (which it was), the reasonable man ideal became important and privileged too.

As the 1950s turned into the 1960s, however, a number of critics began chipping away at the automobile's pedestal. On the international stage, Ralph Nader criticized the traffic safety approach that blamed drivers for accidents; instead, he suggested that the technology itself caused many accidents. In a similar way, Jane Jacobs became the spokesperson for a large movement against automobile-centred urban planning in the United States and Canada, a movement that, in its emphasis on the local, directly challenged the basic principles of high modernism that had dominated urban planning for most of the postwar years and earlier. Vancouverites took up the ideas of both Nader and Jacobs in order to challenge the place of the automobile in their community. They did so most prominently in the late Sixties, when a diverse group of citizens challenged and defeated plans to build a freeway through the city's Chinatown. This type of mid- to late-Sixties criticism represented a significant challenge to (though certainly not a total rejection of) the ideological dominance of automobile-centred high modernism, as well as challenging the experts who told people how to deal with its negative side effects, such as traffic accidents.[5]

What, then, happened to the reasonable man ideal? When automobile-centred high modernism came under attack, what happened to the ideals of masculinity with which it was so bound up? As we shall see, the Sixties criticism of automobile-centred modernity was not just about cars; it was also about the kind of man who sat behind the wheel.

Automophilia

Idealized masculinity could not have been associated with a more important symbol of postwar modernity than the automobile. The car symbolized the central features of postwar modernity: suburbanization, consumption, nuclear family "togetherness," and, most importantly, technological progress.[6] Although the car had been invented in the previous century and mass ownership developed after the Great War, widespread car ownership truly took off after the Second World War.[7] The number of car registrations increased dramatically immediately following the war and continued to increase for much of the postwar years. This increase was partly the result of the city's growing population as more and more migrants (especially from the Prairie provinces) moved to British Columbia. It was also the result of the increased ability of Vancouverites to buy vehicles, as wartime plants converted back to civilian production. With the removal of wartime restrictions on production and consumption, Vancouverites eagerly took to the roads, and in 1946 General Motors placed advertisements in the *Vancouver Sun* apologizing to customers for the slow delivery of ordered vehicles. Claiming that the conversion of plants was still slowing up production, the company promised its customers that it would soon be able to match the high demand.[8]

Beyond the rise in the number of cars (which was significant), there were other developments that suggest a social transformation. Organizations and institutions that were focused on the automobile grew in importance in the postwar years, whether this was the creation of the British Columbia Ministry of Highways in 1955 or the establishment in 1952 of the British Columbia Automobile Association (BCAA) as an organization completely separate from its sister tourism body.[9] The spread of car ownership fed the process of suburbanization that was so characteristic of the era. Earlier Vancouver suburbs had depended on the streetcar; not so the postwar suburbs. Along with new developments in housing construction and home financing, the car was an essential catalyst in the development of a number of suburban areas. The city adopted the car so wholeheartedly that streetcars were abandoned. An entire grid of streetcar lines that had once joined various Vancouver neighbourhoods was replaced between the late 1940s and early 1950s with a trolley-bus service.[10]

Although the car fitted nicely into the era's emphasis on family life and the democratization of modern forms of technology (literally allowing more Canadians to enjoy the benefits of mobility),[11] the individual behind the wheel of a car was largely understood to be a man. As Virginia Schaff has argued about an earlier period, the automobile's promise of power and speed was gendered masculine. Women entered car advertisements largely as objects or symbols of style and elegance. Although families may have used the cars on outings and women may have driven cars, advertisers clearly imagined the typical buyer as a male.[12]

Automobile historian Clay McShane argues that the car served as a kind of masculine getaway from the troubles of the modern world. It offered opportunities for action, adventure, and escape from a bureaucratic and industrialized world.[13] McShane's argument underscores the connection between the automobile and the notion that manhood was threatened by modern life. This notion of masculinity in crisis (and hence in need of an escape) is long-standing, and so are its ironies.[14] Men are presented as needing an escape from modern life even while the very technologies of modernity are being defined in masculine ways. The double-turn tends to hide the real privilege accorded to men by presenting the burdens of authority as victimization. Yet the automobile-as-escape was only the most overt of many ways in which contemporaries associated masculinity with cars. Safety experts such as Bryce defined the ideal driver in the same language as that used to describe the ideal man: responsible, rational, and interested in technology. They presented the reasonable man ideal as the best solution to the dilemmas that the increasing number of cars brought to contemporary life.

Managing Modern Risk

The shiny golden age of the automobile had a rusty underside. The number of car accidents in Vancouver doubled between 1945 and 1950, rising from 3,500 to just over 7,000. Although these numbers levelled off over the following years, they still tended to rise, reaching a high of more than 17,000 in 1968. The number of vehicles involved in accidents showed an even greater increase, going from 6,020 in 1945 to 15,007 in 1949. More Vancouverites crashed their cars with each passing year, while the number of traffic deaths varied from year to year, ranging from a low of twenty-six in 1955 to a high of fifty-one in 1966. Cars may have allowed for the "good life," but they also ended life, and such incidents generated a great deal of attention. Local papers regularly followed the ups and downs of traffic accident and injury numbers, linking small increases and decreases to the success or failure of traffic safety initiatives. On at least one day each week, Vancouverites could pick up their morning paper and see on the front page a story that detailed the car culture's travesty in their own community.[15]

How did Vancouverites respond to automobile accidents? Perhaps not surprisingly, they, like other North Americans, treated car accidents in a very modern way. Safety experts emerged along with the automobile to help explain and deal with its dangers, and they treated car accidents as events that needed to be managed. Just as the automobile itself was a great example of modern control over the environment, its downside seemingly called for an equally modern system of control. Almost uniformly, mid-century safety experts did not aim to control the technological environment. Instead, they called for a greater system of personal control and called on Canadians to adopt a whole new modernist mindset based on risk-management principles.

Safety experts considered it their job to overcome a lack of knowledge about the causes of accidents so that these could be thoroughly known, studied, and ultimately controlled. In this reckoning, car accidents were not dangers to be faced but risks to be managed. Given the car's status as a symbol of the modern in this technologically determinist age, the danger that cars posed was interpreted not as a sign that the technology itself was problematic but as evidence that drivers had not yet learned to become thoroughly modern.

The acceptance of automobile accidents as an unfortunate byproduct of an otherwise useful technology has a long history, dating back at least to the first traffic fatality in New York in 1899. By the postwar years, the anti-car criticism of the early years had subsided under the weight of the automobile's perceived economic, social, and personal benefits. It was simply far easier, as automobile historian Sean O'Connell argues, "for all concerned to place their hope in the claims being made by the emerging 'science' of road safety."[16] This did not mean that car accidents escaped criticism. Quite the opposite – many people felt that car accidents were a grave problem, and a slew of local safety advocates suggested ways to prevent them. But the kinds of people who became interested in the problem and the way in which they spoke about it resulted in a tendency to blame individuals rather than technology. No one seriously suggested reducing the number of cars as a way of reducing the number of accidents. Safety work was always about making the car more palatable and about easing its place into everyday life. Safety advocates were car advocates.[17]

Industries and individuals with a vested interest in boosting the car's public image dominated the main local safety organization, the Vancouver Traffic and Safety Council (VTSC). Although the VTSC later included domestic safety under its mandate, it largely concerned itself with the problem of traffic accidents. Directors and members included representatives from such organizations as BC Motor Transportation Ltd., the BC Motor Dealers Association, BC Electric, the Vancouver Board of Trade, the Downtown Business Association, the BCAA, the Taxicab Owners' Association, and McKinley's Driving School. In this way, the VTSC was similar to the national safety organization, the Canadian Highway Safety Council (CHSC), which was founded in 1954 and also was controlled by automobile-related business interests.

In Vancouver, a VTSC representative sat on the city's Official Traffic Commission (OTC), a municipal board set up to deal with all local traffic issues. Other safety officials who sat on this board included the city engineer, the chief constable, the city solicitor, aldermen, and representatives from the BCAA and the Downtown Business Association. The organizations that typically appeared before the OTC to speak on traffic matters included the Board of Trade, the Junior Board of Trade, the local Council of Women, and parent-teacher organizations. More broadly, the British Columbia Medical Association, political parties, and the federal and provincial governments all, in greater and lesser capacities, spoke on the phenomenon of car accidents in Vancouver.

What is striking is not only that corporations and government boosters dominated car safety expertise, a subject already neatly outlined by Ralph Nader, but also the way in which they did so – specifically, their claim that the solution lay in the achievement of a new kind of human mastery over technology. Experts used a variety of devices to drive this point home, to convince drivers to take control of the automobile. One of the more popular tactics was to compare the automobile to a wild animal that needed taming. "A lion in the streets knows nothing of the rules of civilized behaviour," claimed Ethel McClellan. "But when a human being takes his place behind the wheel it becomes the most dangerous killer at large in our modern world." Mixing his metaphors, J.C. Furnas made the same point in his much-cited *Reader's Digest* article: "The automobile is treacherous, just as a cat is. It is tragically difficult to realize that it can become the deadliest missile. As enthusiasts tell you, it makes 65 feel like nothing at all. But 65 an hour is 100 feet a second, a speed which puts a viciously unjustified responsibility on brakes and human reflexes, and can instantly turn this docile luxury into a mad bull elephant." Here Furnas presented the car as a cat, a missile, and an elephant. All these threats, he claimed, needed to be tamed, to be put to good use by the car experts' vision of the ideal modern citizen / circus ringmaster.[18]

Although they used animal metaphors, safety advocates went to great lengths to convince drivers that the problem they faced was modern. They worried that modernity created a sense of ease that minimized vigilance. The *Canadian Motorist* warned that this "push-button attitude" could make drivers "act like a machine – unthinkingly." British Columbia's superintendent of motor vehicles, George Hood, blamed the postwar rise in car accidents not on the increased number of cars on the road but on the problems of individual drivers: "Until such time as every motor-vehicle driver and pedestrian accepts his personal responsibility to obey the rules and regulations made for the purpose of protecting life and property, we shall continue to have this wanton loss." Almost twenty years later, Sam Kershaw, executive director of the British Columbia Safety Council, expressed the same sentiments. "The problem," he argued, "is man's behaviour in the mechanical age ... The realization that an automobile even at its best is a fast, powerful, inanimate machine, guided only by the judgment and control of the man behind the wheel, is proof enough that traffic accidents are thus as preventable as the individual driver wants or knows how to make them."[19]

Drivers needed to be excessively rational and aware to keep their attention tuned to all the latest gadgets and instruments. The automobile was a delicate instrument that called for a delicate touch. "In this very delicacy of touch," one safety advocate warned, "lies the danger of wavering of attention. We have definitely arrived at the era of finger-tip control in cars, but a keener mentality is required if safety is the end product." As a solution, he argued that drivers needed to become thoroughly engaged with their cars. They needed to blend the technological and the psychological, the car and the mind. Safe driving meant monitoring the many gauges and buttons so that you not only drove safely but also could enjoy what he called the "thrill of performance."[20]

This blend of modernist subjectivity and technological performance came across clearly in the key mantra of traffic safety experts: the "three E's." The experts argued that if enough steps were taken on each of these E's – engineering, education, and enforcement – traffic accidents could be eliminated. Although ostensibly about three different methods of achieving the same goal, the three E's shared a common ideology that blamed accidents on the individual (on the so-called "human factor") and attempted to inculcate the proper modernist subjectivity to overcome the human faults.

Writing on the first of the three E's – engineering – demonstrated the broad faith in automotive technology in the postwar years. Engineering safety meant attending to the design of cities and cars in creating and preventing accidents, including such things as the role of street signs, parking meters, one-way streets, and steering systems. The engineering of car safety was largely the realm of engineers and the technically minded, especially Kenneth Vaughan-Birch, Vancouver's city engineer. He advised Vancouver's OTC on a steady course of incremental changes, including the provision of parking meters in 1946, the development of more one-way streets, and a slow increase in the number of traffic lights, stop signs, and pedestrian crosswalks. Like other municipal engineers, Vaughan-Birch tried to balance the desire for free-flowing and speedy movement against safety concerns and local interests. The OTC managed the car accident problem at the micro level: parents who complained of unsafe intersections for their children; businesses that wanted special parking measures that would interrupt traffic flow; residents near dangerous intersections who wanted traffic lights. Against these calls for more regulation, the OTC sought to achieve its main goal, maximum traffic flow.[21]

When Vancouver officials looked at the car itself, they tended to do so only as another way to get at drivers. Before cars could be licensed in Vancouver, they needed to pass a safety inspection. Vancouver's safety officials prided themselves on the city's inspection station, a rare institution in these years and one that became provincewide in 1964. Such an emphasis on the role of the vehicle itself in the accident problem was uncommon in Canada and seemed to be a significant innovation. Yet the station was not as radical as some claimed. It merely tested individual upkeep of the car, not the safety of the technology itself, and thus assumed that cars were safe when they came out of the factory. Whenever safety officials debated the cause of car accidents, they could – and did – argue that it was not the cars themselves that caused accidents in Vancouver; after all, the cars had passed inspection.[22]

Engineering features that made cars safer – such as seat belts or collapsible steering columns – were the realm of science fiction and idealistic futurism, a hoped-for possibility that might someday make life better but could not be expected right away. Seat belts for cars were almost unheard of until well into the 1950s, and companies did not begin to put them regularly in cars until the early 1960s. A 1952 *Maclean's* article quoted an executive of the Automobile Dealer

Associations of Canada on the idea of putting safety belts in all cars: "Never heard of such an idea. People would get the idea that automobiles are as dangerous as planes. They'd be afraid to buy cars."[23] And they did not need to be afraid because cars were safe.

In 1957 an official with the Canadian Highway Safety Council claimed that "today's motor car is about as safe as it can be made."[24] Articles on possible new safety features inevitably ended by claiming that they would be for naught unless individual drivers changed their attitude. Companies were benevolent overseers who wanted to make cars safer but were constrained by costs, technology, and the ever-important consumer, who simply did not want new features that looked funny, made for awkward driving, or were simply too expensive.[25] A 1959 *Maclean's* article on eight ways to reduce traffic accidents did not mention engineering at all.[26] So little criticism was directed at the car that in 1964, one year before Ralph Nader showed the dangers of the Chevrolet Corvair, *Canadian Motorist* gave the car a glowing review, mentioning safety not at all. The Corvair was, according to the magazine's reviewer, "a car to delight the hearts of those motorists (bless them) who still believe that motoring can be fun."[27]

The other two E's, education and enforcement, picked up where engineering left off, moving right to the individual and trying to inculcate the proper modernist approach to technological risk. Education was the first weapon in the battle against car accidents, and battlefronts included exhibits by the VTSC at annual events such as the Pacific International Motor Show and the Pacific National Exhibition. There were traffic safety drives sponsored by the police and advertised in local newspapers, safe driver pledges, and leaflets handed out by the Junior Board of Trade. The BCAA, VTSC, and the provincial Department of Motor Vehicles showed safety films and gave talks to schools and community groups. Many officials wrote articles in local papers and national magazines explaining that the "human factor" caused almost all accidents. Children came in for special attention, with school safety patrol programs and traffic education held in local parks on miniature streets. Local groups called for the retesting of all drivers and for pedestrian education, especially for the very old and the young. But it was high school driver education – the one program that never came into being – that safety advocates truly wanted. Whenever the accident toll took a turn for the worse, this was the default solution. Private companies, including the local McKinley Driving School, a longtime supporter of the VTSC, offered courses to all Vancouverites. Yet this was not sufficient. If only there were universal driver education courses in the schools, said the safety advocates, accident numbers would really drop.[28]

Educational boosters saw their work as a kind of civilizing process. In his speech to the 1956 VTSC annual meeting, Vancouver Alderman H.D. Wilson asked: "What happens to us when we get into our cars and take over the job of driving? It would appear that many of us lose our powers of reasoning completely. How many of us become ill-mannered, boorish, impatient, irritable – almost all of those characteristics which we dislike in others and, under ordinary circumstances, control within ourselves? Why can't we be drivers and normal people at one and the same time?"[29] The VTSC used education as a way of teaching self-control and responsibility. And while both men and women could be responsible, the concept was of special importance for postwar men. Psychologists linked the achievement of responsibility with the achievement of manhood. According to such advice, men were to accept the responsibilities of breadwinning, give up the wayward days of bachelorhood and youth, and become men in the process.[30]

This emphasis on responsibility translated well into public policy over car accidents. Throughout the 1940s and 1950s the government sought ways to ensure that drivers were financially responsible, that they either had insurance or had sufficient money to pay for any damages caused by their accidents. This goal spurred on the British Columbia Department of Motor Vehicles to establish its first Drivers' Education Division in 1953.[31] This was not driver education as it might be conceived conventionally; it was more retributive than preventive. It targeted "habitual offenders" and "accident prone" drivers. The department formally reviewed their records and either sent warning letters or suspended their licences. The institution of these measures put administrative force and a regulatory apparatus behind the need to be responsible.

The last of the three E's – enforcement – picked up on this retributive element. Legal measures were, as one VTSC member called them, "education by enforcement."[32] Pamphlets and newspaper campaigns were the carrot of accident prevention, and tickets and criminal sanctions were the stick. Of course, other motives guided some enforcement enthusiasts. It is hard not to see the institutional will of the police (a desire for more resources and more power) behind the almost continual call for more traffic officers. Police forces used the automobile to get resources, and they were in turn transformed by the need to police the automobile.[33] Yet these bureaucratic desires coexisted with a belief in the individualistic nature of the problem and the desire to regulate behaviour to fit the demands of modern technology. Those who advocated enforcement believed that if only the bad drivers could be stopped – if only the bad human spark plugs could be replaced – the engine of progress would run smoothly.

The main villain in the safety debate was the drunk driver. The postwar years saw a consistent campaign on the part of many safety advocates to smear drunk drivers, those considered to play the largest role in creating accidents. Safety advocates had a tough job. Drinking and driving, at least in moderation, was not seen as a significant problem. Even early attempts to stop drinking and driving still allowed for consumption, with the amount depending on the type of alcohol. The law also made distinctions based on the amount consumed. Two offences existed: one for driving while intoxicated, the most serious offence, and another for driving while impaired. Lawmakers debated the need for two offences but maintained the distinction throughout this period because they believed that juries would let too many drunk drivers free if a guilty verdict meant jail time.

Then there was the question of how to measure drunkenness. In the early postwar years, the law relied on the judgment of police and other witnesses. Did they believe the driver was drunk? If so, how seriously? Because of the unreliability of this method, there were very few convictions for either category of drunk driving, especially when compared with how much of a role safety advocates believed it played; contemporary estimates linked alcohol to anywhere from 30 to 90 percent of all accidents. Something had to be done. The police wanted to use scientific tests, machines that could measure drunkenness at the site of an accident. Vancouver police began using a tool called the Drunkometer in 1953, and the Breathalyzer was first introduced in

Canada in 1956. But the law treated this evidence skeptically. Courts did not accept test results as definite proof; they could only corroborate other evidence. Furthermore, drivers could refuse to take the tests.[34]

Drinking and driving became a problem because of the extent to which drinking made rational risk-management behaviour harder to achieve. Since at least the mid-nineteenth century, drink had been a significant symbol in discussions of civilized behaviour, especially modern manly behaviour. Being able to handle one's liquor appropriately was linked to the achievement of manhood. Earlier temperance and women's activists had based their appeals on the fact that many men could not meet these ideals and that women suffered as a result. The drunk driver discourse served as a modern way of continuing these discussions. Drinking's effect on one's ability to be modern was significant. The British Columbia Medical Association (BCMA) warned that alcohol made a particularly bad mix with driving because drinking robbed people of their most civilized skills. The BCMA claimed that there was a drinking cycle in which social skills were lost one by one, with those learned most recently (such as driving) going first. "In this progression of events," the BCMA argued, "the effects on the functions concerned with safe driving, such as co-ordination, judgement, self discipline, and control" would be taken away by only a few drinks.[35] In other words, drinking could steal a driver's modernity.

What is striking is the way that the drunk driver and other "problem drivers" matched the usual bogeymen in the closet of postwar manhood. Although safety experts frequently claimed that anyone could be in an accident, they nonetheless tarred bad drivers with characteristics considered to be unmanly. The "hit and run driver" was a case in point. In 1962 Hal Tennant warned Canadians about the dangers of identifying too closely with this figure by thinking that anyone could be in the situation of needing or wanting to escape from the scene of an accident. It appears he thought philandering was the common excuse and expected his readers to sympathize with the driver who rushed off for fear of being caught at infidelity. But he said that this kind of thinking could not be sustained. In the "automobile age," Tennant warned, "nice guys never run away."[36] The *Vancouver Province* agreed with Tennant's assessment. It reported 1,508 accidents in 1959 and claimed that the most common reasons for leaving included impairment, driving without a licence or insurance, having someone else's wife in the car, or driving a stolen vehicle. The paper also noted that it could be just plain panic, a sure sign that one had not maintained self-control.[37]

This controlled and disciplined citizenship could not just be assumed; it had to be achieved. In the 1940s and 1950s the figure of the juvenile delinquent served as a lightning rod for Canadians' fears that this discipline was endangered. While the female delinquent garnered concern for her sexual behaviour, the male came under scrutiny for his inability to contain his aggression and be responsible.[38] This made the male juvenile delinquent an easy target for safety advocates. D.G. Dainton blamed accidents on poor young drivers who drove recklessly and did not care if they got into an accident because they had a cheap car. This kind of driver, Dainton argued, "has no position of responsibility, either in a job or in the community ... He drives recklessly, devil-may-care, flouting the highway code, and expecting everyone, motorists and pedestrians, to give him right of way at all times. Everything he does when driving leads to accidents."[39] Dainton directly connected social responsibility with driving responsibility, and the process of becoming a man with the task of good driving.

The gendered nature of traffic safety discourse becomes clear when we compare it with postwar ideas of masculinity and femininity. In giving his account of the differences between the sexes, Benjamin Spock, the most popular child-rearing expert of the postwar years, described young boys in a way that matched the ideals of the safety experts. He claimed that boys instinctively expressed a "love of machines and gadgets for their own sake." Robbed of the ability to bear children, he maintained, men expressed creativity in such things as building model planes and scooters and "designing futuristic automobiles and planes." The "urge to play at being fierce and intrusive comes more naturally to most boys" because they are more aggressive. Spock linked these traits to risk taking: "Most men and boys seem to be courting danger a lot of the time ... It's boys who go out too far on thin ice and climb cliffs and it's men who take risks in boats and cars ... For a man a car is a symbol of his ambition to be a powerful person: in reaching his goals, in competing with other men, in impressing women."[40] Another Canadian psychologist suggested that it was fathers who taught "rational judgment" and "logical thinking."[41] Spock and other experts claimed that, when properly controlled, boys' natural proclivity for rational action, creative engineering, and taking risks helped them to become men. This same development – the achievement of balance between risk taking and risk management – also just happened to be the safety experts' preferred solution to the traffic safety problem.

Ralph Nader, Radicalism, and the Critique of Manly Modernism

The VTSC, *Canadian Motorist*, and others presented technological problems such as car accidents as a failure to be fully modern. From this perspective, the rise in the number of car crashes represented not a problem with the technology but a sign that drivers had not yet fully adopted a sufficiently modernist mindset. And so their work in the 1940s and 1950s consisted of engineering, educating, and enforcing this type of driver. Even during the 1950s, however, alternative currents of thought suggested different ways of understanding traffic accidents, technology, and the modernist project more generally.[42] In the mid-1960s, such alternatives coalesced into a radical challenge to high-modernist thinking about technology and to the gender ideals that went along with it. A growing number of critics noted the negative attributes of modern expertise, its often one-sided inability to see the fullness of life, its disciplinary chafing, and the effect this had on communities and individuals. In essence, Sixties critics of modernization picked up on the earlier concern that the system was out of whack, and they shifted the balance, opting for less certainty and reason, more risk taking, and less risk management.

The publication of Ralph Nader's *Unsafe at Any Speed* in November 1965 cracked open the fissures in the debate over car accidents. It is often unwise to accord any one person or event too much significance, yet Nader seems to deserve it. After 1965, you could hardly talk about car safety or car accidents without discussing – or refusing to discuss – Ralph Nader.[43] In *Unsafe at Any Speed*, he reversed the logic of what he called the "safety establishment" – the claim that drivers caused most accidents. He argued that automobile makers wanted the public to blame drivers for accidents when in fact the car was really to blame. Cars were designed to be dangerous. At the very least, they were not designed to be safe. In *Unsafe at Any Speed*, Nader gave repeated examples of automobile makers covering up mistakes that endangered drivers' lives. Moreover, he argued that the companies dominated the safety establishment, turning its critique away from car design; he held that the companies also dominated the engineering and standard-setting professions; that very little science on the safety of cars was done; and that, in the end, stylistic details overrode concerns about safety. In essence, Nader claimed that the automobile makers managed a cover-up of phenomenal proportions, one that turned the public's eye away from the real cause of traffic injuries: car design.

Nader not only criticized what he called the "safety establishment," but he also found fault with the kind of men who promoted the driver-focused safety consensus. He criticized the safety advocates' technology-focused, bureaucratic form of modern manliness. He populated *Unsafe at Any Speed* with men who failed to act because they allowed their knowledge of what was right to be subsumed by their company's interests. In essence, their loyalty to company, technology, and the higher cause of automobile-centred modernity meant that they refused to acknowledge the dangers of the automobile. Nader quoted a Chrysler executive who told the 1965 graduating class of the Lawrence Institute of Technology that "a prime requisite for getting ahead in industry is identification of your personal objectives with the objectives of the company."[44] This picked up directly from fears of the Organization Man which had been so prominent in the 1950s – the sense that bureaucratic suburban life had disastrous consequences for modern manhood.[45] At the same time as he criticized the main symbol of postwar modernity, Nader also criticized the ideal of masculinity with which it was associated: modern manliness.

Nader's critique of automotive technology and its makers spread to Canada and Vancouver. The BCMA drew directly from Nader to express its own frustration with automobile companies. "One has only to read the recent book *Unsafe at Any Speed* by Ralph Nader," the association reported in 1966, "to realize the 'designed-in-dangers' of the North American car. One simply cannot buy a relatively safe car made in North America ... The car manufacturers seem only to be interested in sales and in designing eye catching ornamental, super speed missiles."[46] The BCMA's Traffic and Safety Committee had initially been created to determine guidelines for medically unfit drivers, a task that had them focusing exclusively on the individual's role in car accidents. Yet the committee gradually expanded its focus to the point where it advocated the mandatory introduction of seat belts, child restraints, and the use of helmets for motorcyclists.[47]

Those who still held to the older safety consensus now presented themselves as embattled by the forces of unreason. If others attacked the benevolence of modern technology, these experts found shelter behind the ideal trait of manly modernism: reasoned objectivity. In 1965 *Canadian Motorist* complained that a great deal of "criticism, some of it unmercifully vitriolic, is being hurled at the automobile manufacturers these days." The magazine particularly disliked the tone of the criticism and called for "a reasoned approach to the problem, no brickbats of blame, no self-conscious sloganeering."[48] This was the modernist return to rationality against the emotionalism of its critics. Phil Gaglardi, British Columbia's minister of highways, was characteristically even more direct. "When Nader tries to tell the United States of America that automobiles are more unsafe than anything else," he told a meeting of police chiefs, "I say he's a nut." Returning to the individualistic theme that so dominated postwar safety expertise, Gaglardi claimed, "It takes 10,000 nuts to hold an automobile together but just one behind the wheel to disintegrate it."[49] Here Gaglardi brought it back to sanity and reason. To criticize the car, so this line of thinking went, was itself a crazy act.

Yet it was an increasingly popular form of madness. While Nader and others questioned the car, a number of Vancouverites went further and began to challenge automobile-centred and expert-led urban planning. In the postwar years, the growth of many cities in North American had been shaped by modernist urban planning that called for the removal of urban "blight," the redevelopment of such areas with the extension of large-scale social housing, and the building of freeways to facilitate traffic flow into and out of the city to expanding suburban areas. The United States led the way in this type of development, but similar schemes garnered the support of officials in Vancouver by the late 1950s. In many respects, Vancouver was a logical match for these urban planners. In the 1930s, centrist and right-wing political forces had come together at the municipal level to block the left from taking control of city council. The resulting party, the Non-Partisan Association (NPA), governed the city for the next thirty years. The NPA established a bureaucratic form of expert government that gave free reign to administrators and their plans.[50]

Two different schemes of these planners came together in the Sixties to force a re-evaluation of this kind of modernist planning. The first was an urban renewal scheme that sought to remove urban blight from the area just to the east of the downtown core, an area that included Chinatown. The second was a plan to build a freeway through the centre of the city and directly through Chinatown. Both plans would have dislocated thousands of residents, many of them Chinese, and led to the destruction of a huge section of one of Vancouver's oldest areas. While two phases of the urban renewal scheme had gone ahead in the early Sixties, a collection of different Vancouverites banded together in 1967 to defeat the freeway plan. .

The anti-urban renewal movement of the Sixties represented a significant challenge to modernist planning and to the notion that development worked best when led by experts alone. The way in which activists voiced their discontent was significant. They drew upon the anti-Organization Man rhetoric of men who had been frustrated by their experiences with the modernist project in the 1950s. The anti-freeway activists included in their critical repertoire an attack on the kind of men who were behind urban planning in Vancouver. They especially disliked the "bureaucrats" and "authoritarians" at city hall and in the city engineering department.[51] Activists urged a more participatory democratic decision-making process in urban planning. They presented the male heroes of postwar modernization – bureaucrats, engineers, and planners – as the villains thwarting their quest for a more involved democracy.

Vancouverites and other North Americans who fought similar urban redevelopment schemes could look to Jane Jacobs, whose book, *The Death and Life of Great American Cities* (1961), offered an alternative vision of urban planning. Jacobs eloquently outlined the inadequacies of modernist design that sought to impose automobile-inspired order. She argued that cities were being made unlivable by an expertise that privileged visual and aesthetic order over the actual messy orderliness of real life. She also challenged the idea that cities and citizens should continuously make way for more roads and cars, arguing that building more roads would only lead to their being filled by more cars. Commentators have noted the gendered nature of Jacobs's ideas. The anthropologist James Scott argues that the bird's-eye view style of planning came mostly from male planners who did not have roots in the actual communities and lives of those who lived there. But as a woman, Jacobs spent more time at home watching the neighbourhood. She could see its development first-hand, learn its rules and practices, and then base her critique on this lived experience. While it may be true that a man could have come up with a similar type of critique (and some did), her analysis was certainly gendered. Given the strong link between modernist planning, automobiles, and masculinity in the postwar years, her challenge had gendered repercussions; like Nader and the Vancouver anti-freeway activists, Jacobs's work challenged the common-sense status of modernist knowledge and the gendered hierarchies that went along with it.[52]

o—o—o

In 1943 Leonard Marsh released his famous *Report on Social Security*, which has been heralded as the cornerstone of the postwar Canadian welfare state. Although most of its suggestions did not immediately come out in government policy, the report nevertheless captured public attention as the Canadian version of the Beveridge Report, the British plan for postwar reconstruction. Marsh offered a gendered reconstruction vision aimed at getting men back into their place as breadwinners and ensuring a successful economic transition in which wartime hopes and demands for greater social justice received their just rewards in government policy. He also represented a vision of expert-led governance in which a number of social planners in Ottawa and other centres would guide social policy and bureaucratic practice.[53] Less well known, but equally important for Vancouverites, is another report that Marsh published six years later. Having moved to the University of British Columbia, he conducted a study of urban blight in Vancouver. In 1949 he published his study, *Rebuilding a Neighbour-*

hood, in which he called for an urban renewal scheme for the city, focusing especially on the eastern side of the downtown core, the area including Chinatown. Marsh's plans did not see immediate action, but they were later the inspiration for the city's urban renewal scheme. It was this scheme that many Vancouverites organized against – and defeated the final stages of – in the late 1960s.

The different fates accorded to the two 1940s Marsh reports nicely capture the changes in attitude towards automobile-centred modernity and ideas of masculinity that occurred in the next two decades. The first report represents the origins of postwar planning and optimistic expert-led development. It looked forward to a postwar period in which a social security system, organized by rational planners, would support a nation of breadwinners. Although many aspects of the report were not implemented (at least, not immediately), its ideals of masculinity were carried forward in the postwar celebration of responsible breadwinning as the hallmark of manhood. But when Marsh's second report finally began to be implemented in the Sixties, something had begun to change. A new range of critics had emerged who were more eager to challenge modernist planning and the style of manhood it celebrated. A variety of individuals and groups, ranging from the famous (Ralph Nader and Jane Jacobs) to the local (Setty Pendakur and the Chinese Benevolent Association), argued that the experts did not actually have the best interests of all in mind. Couching their arguments in a language of participatory democracy and anti-authoritarianism, the car critics and anti-freeway activists challenged the notion that these experts were working for the universal good. Was not the problem, they asked, the masculinity of the experts themselves – too obsessed with control and rational manipulation and less caring about human interaction and community participation? Perhaps the Organization Man was not to be pitied; he was to be feared.

When historians discuss the revolutionary changes in gender relations in the Sixties, they usually dwell on such topics as the sexual revolution, the increase in married women workers, rising divorce rates, and the generational conflicts of the baby boomers.[54] However, the changes to ideas about what makes a good man also had their origins in other, less overtly gendered transformations. By the middle years of the twentieth century the very language of masculinity had became embedded in the practices of modern life. That being a good man and a good driver were similar achievements seemed not worth mentioning; it could simply be assumed. However, when critics attacked the benefits of this modern technology and its experts in the Sixties, their attack also affected the ideals of masculinity bound up with this modernist vision. The change is perhaps clarified if we return to W.A. Bryce's speech with which we began. In 1960 Bryce could pass off a mangled version of Rudyard Kipling as the answer to traffic safety; by the end of the decade, there were plenty of critics around to tell him it was nothing more than bad poetry.

NOTES

1 W.A. Bryce, "Luck or Calculated Risk?" *Vancouver Traffic and Safety Council Annual Report* (hereafter VTSC annual report), 1960, Vancouver City Archives (VCA), Mayor's Office fond, 36-E-2, file 129.

2 Ibid.

3 Nancy Christie, *Engendering the State: Family, Work, and Welfare in Canada* (Toronto: University of Toronto Press, 2000); Ruth Roach Pierson, "Gender and the Unemployment Insurance Debates in Canada, 1934–1940," *Labour/Le Travail* 25 (1990): 77–103; Chris Dummitt, "Finding a Place for Father: Selling the Barbecue in Postwar Canada," *Journal of the Canadian Historical Association* 9 (1998): 209–23; Veronica Strong-Boag, "Home Dreams: Women and the Suburban Experiment in Canada, 1945–1960," *Canadian Historical Review* 72, no. 4 (1991): 471–504; Robert Rutherdale, "Fatherhood, Masculinity, and the Good Life during Canada's Baby Boom, 1945–1965," *Journal of Family History* 24, no. 3 (1999): 351–73.

4 The modern version of the reasonable man dates from the rise of the capitalist middle class during the Industrial Revolution. This class insisted on its superior ability to be sober financial leaders, and its members demonstrated these traits in their style of masculine and feminine comportment. See Leonore Davidoff and Catherine Hall, *Family Fortunes: Men and Women of the English Middle Class, 1780–1850* (Chicago: University of Chicago Press, 1987).

5 Ralph Nader, *Unsafe at Any Speed: The Designed-in Dangers of the American Automobile* (New York: Grossman, 1965); Jane Jacobs, *The*

Death and Life of Great American Cities (New York: Random House, 1961).

6 On technological determinism and the respect for the modern more generally, see Pam Roper, "The Limits of Laissez-innover: Canada's Automation Controversy, 1955–1969," *Journal of Canadian Studies* 34, no. 3 (1999): 88. For a different perspective based on Canadian attitudes towards domestic goods, see Joy Parr, *Domestic Goods: The Material, the Moral, and the Economic in the Postwar Years* (Toronto: University of Toronto Press, 1999).

7 American historians frequently refer to the period after the Second World War and before the late Sixties as the "golden age" of the automobile. See David Thoms, Len Holden, and Tim Claydon, eds., *The Motor Car and Popular Culture in the Twentieth Century* (Aldershot: Ashgate, 1998); James J. Flink, *The Automobile Age* (Cambridge, Mass.: MIT Press, 1988); John Jerome, *The Death of the Automobile: The Fatal Effect of the Golden Era, 1955–1970* (New York: W.W. Norton, 1972); James E. Vance, Jr, *Capturing the Horizon: The Historical Geography of Transportation since the Sixteenth Century* (Baltimore & London: Johns Hopkins University Press, 1986).

8 For statistics on car registrations, see *Annual Report of the Department of Motor Vehicles* (Victoria: King's Printer, 1945–49), and *Annual Report of the Motor Vehicle Branch* (Victoria: King's Printer, 1950–70). On Vancouver's growing population in the postwar years, see Jean Barman, *The West Beyond the West: A History of British Columbia* (Toronto: University of Toronto Press, 1991), 273.

9 "Protecting the Motorist," *Vancouver Province*, 17 January 1952, 4.

10 The filling in of Vancouver is nicely visualized in Bruce MacDonald, *Vancouver: A Visual History* (Vancouver: Talon Books, 1992). On suburbanization, see Richard Harris and Peter J. Larkham, eds., *Changing Suburbs: Foundation, Form, and Function* (New York: Routledge, 1999). On the gender dynamics of this suburbanization, see Strong-Boag, "Home Dreams." On the relation between automobiles and suburbanization, see Kenneth T. Jackson, *Crabgrass Frontier: The Suburbanization of the United States* (New York: Oxford University Press, 1985). On urban transportation changes in Vancouver, see Henry Ewert, *The Story of the B.C. Electric Railway Company* (North Vancouver: Whitecap Books, 1986)

11 On the family orientation of the era, see Douglas Owram, *Born at the Right Time: A History of the Baby Boom Generation* (Toronto: University of Toronto Press, 1996). On the link between technological modernity

and the automobile, see Wolfgang Sachs, *For Love of the Automobile: Looking Back into the History of Our Desires*, trans. Don Reneau (Berkeley: University of California Press, 1992).

12 Virginia Scharff, "Gender, Electricity, and Automobility," in *The Car and the City: The Automobile, the Built Environment, and Daily Urban Life*, ed. Martin Wachs and Margaret Crawford, 75–85 (Ann Arbor: University of Michigan Press, 1992).

13 Clay McShane, *Down the Asphalt Path: The Automobile and the American City* (New York: Columbia University Press, 1994), 152–3.

14 Much of the early work on the history of masculinity dealt with this issue of masculinity in crisis. See Michael Roper and John Tosh, eds., *Manful Assertions: Masculinities in Britain since 1800* (London: Routledge, 1991), and Mark Carnes and Clyde Griffen, eds., *Meanings for Manhood: Construction of Masculinity in Victorian America* (Chicago: University of Chicago Press, 1990).

15 The number of car accidents in Vancouver during this period are drawn from *Annual Report of the Department of Motor Vehicles* (Victoria: King's Printer, 1945–49) and *Annual Report of the Motor Vehicle Branch* (Victoria: King's Printer, 1950–70).

16 Sean O'Connell *The Car in British Society: Class, Gender, and Motoring, 1896–1939* (Manchester: Manchester University Press, 1998), 143–4. See also, McShane, *Down the Asphalt Path*, chapter 9.

17 My assessment of Vancouver's safety advocates in these paragraphs is based on a reading of the minutes of the city's Official Traffic Commission and the annual reports, select records of the Vancouver Traffic and Safety Council, and the articles published in local, provincial, and national publications by traffic safety advocates, all of which are quoted directly to prove more specific points below.

18 Ethel McLellan, "A Lion in the Streets," *Canadian Motorist*, November 1958, 5–6; J.C. Furnas, "And Sudden Death," in *Reader's Digest*, reprinted in *Trades and Labor Congress Journal*, 25, no. 9 (1946): 42–4.

19 *Annual Report of the Department of Motor Vehicles* (Victoria: King's Printer, 1945), 19; S.C. Kershaw, "Driver Education: Essence of Road Safety," BC *Motorist*, 3, no. 5 (1964).

20 "Automation and the Human Approach," *Canadian Motorist*, October–November 1959, 3; George R. Jackson, "Don't Overdrive Your Car," *Canadian Motorist*, November 1958, 8.

21 See minutes of the Vancouver OTC for this period. For more on the role of traffic engineers in automobile safety, see McShane, *Down the Asphalt Path*, chapter 10.

22 "Drivers Blamed for 99 Pct. of Crashes," *Vancouver Sun*, 5 January 1949; Bill Fletcher, *Vancouver Sun*, 28 October 1958. This is the irony in discussions of engineering car safety during the period: the car companies created the very standards against which they could be judged. So long as cars matched up with how safe the company said cars could be, the technology was deemed to be safe. See, Jerry L. Mashaw and David L. Harfst, *The Struggle for Auto Safety* (Cambridge, Mass.: Harvard University Press, 1990), chapter 2.

23 Fred Bodsworth, "How to Live Through a Crash," *Maclean's*, 1 October 1952, 10–11, 55, 57–9.

24 Marcus Van Steen, "Slogans Won't Stop the Highway Slaughter," *Canadian Business*, September 1957, 138–48.

25 VTSC annual report, 1962, VCA, Office of the City Clerk, series 40, 120-C-2, file 148; Robert Johnston, "Temperature Plays Tricks on Your Car," *Canadian Motorist*, June 1958, 4; George R. Jackson, "Don't Overdrive Your Car," *Canadian Motorist*, November 1958, 8.

26 Sidney Katz, "8 Ways to Cut Traffic Deaths," *Maclean's*, 28 February 1959, 13–14, 53–5.

27 "Corvair Monza," *Canadian Motorist*, June 1964, 20.

28 On the safety advocates' education plans, see, for example, VTSC, various documents, VCA, Office of the City Clerk, series 20, 19-D-4, file 6; comments by each superintendent of motor vehicles for British Columbia, in BC Motor Vehicle Branch and Department of Motor Vehicle annual reports for the period; *British Columbia Automobile Association Annual Report*, 1958, BCAA Archives, box A-19, file 1.

29 VTSC annual report, 1956, VCA, Mayor's Office fonds, 35-F-3, file 16.

30 On advice to men, see Mona Gleason, *Normalizing the Ideal: Psychology, Schooling, and the Family in Postwar Canada* (Toronto: University of Toronto Press, 1999), 66–71; Robert Griswold, *Fatherhood in America: A History* (New York: Basic Books, 1993), chapter 9.

31 *Annual Report of the Motor Vehicle Branch*, 1953 (Victoria: King's Printer, 1954).

32 VTSC annual report, 1956, VCA, Mayor's Office fonds, 35-F-3, file 16.

33 On the transformation of one Canadian police force as a result of the automobile, see John Weaver, *Crimes, Constables, and Courts: Order and Transgression in a Canadian City, 1816–1970* (Montreal & Kingston: McGill-Queen's University Press, 1995).

34 "City Police Begin Drunkometer Use," *Vancouver Sun*, 28 October 1953; "The Cup That Kills," *Canadian Motorist*, January–February 1967, 12–14; the debates on 22 April 1947 and at various points in February and

April 1954, Canada, House of Commons, *Debates*, 1947, 1954. See also Joseph R. Gusfield, *The Culture of Public Problems: Drinking-Driving and the Symbolic Order* (Chicago: University of Chicago Press, 1981).

35 "Alcohol and Driving: A Renewed Appeal For Action," *British Columbia Medical Journal* 6, no. 3 (1964). On gender and drinking in other contexts, see Robert Campbell, *"Sit Down and Drink Your Beer": Regulating Vancouver's Beer Parlours, 1925–1954* (Toronto: University of Toronto Press, 2001); Jan Noel, *Canada Dry: Temperance Crusades before Confederation* (Toronto: University of Toronto Press, 1995); Mariana Valverde, *The Age of Light, Soap, and Water: Moral Reform in English Canada, 1885–1925* (Toronto: McClelland & Stewart, 1991).

36 Hal Tennant, "The Public Crime," *Maclean's*, 10 February 1962, 16–17.

37 "1,508 Hit-Run Accidents in 1959," *Vancouver Province*, 4 June 1960, 1.

38 On juvenile delinquency, see Mary Louise Adams, *The Trouble with Normal: Postwar Youth and the Making of Heterosexuality* (Toronto: University of Toronto Press, 1997), and Franca Iacovetta, "Gossip, Contest, and Power in the Making of Suburban Bad Girls: Toronto 1945–1960," *Canadian Historical Review* 80, no. 4 (1999): 585–623.

39 D.G. Dainton, "Concerning Automobile Accidents," *Saturday Night*, 18 March 1961, 54.

40 Elsewhere in the article, Spock railed against feminists who were "resentful of men's advantages." See Benjamin Spock, "Some Differences between the Sexes," in Spock, *Problems of Parents* (Boston: Houghton Mifflin, 1960), 121–8. On the advice of Canadian parenting experts for the same period, see Gleason, *Normalizing the Ideal*.

41 M. Prados, "On Promoting Mental Health," *Canadian Psychiatric Association Journal* 2 (1957), 36–51, as cited in Gleason, *Normalizing the Ideal*, 69.

42 Margot A. Henrickson, *Dr. Strangelove's America: Society and Culture in the Atomic Age* (Berkeley & Los Angeles: University of California Press, 1997); Alan Nadel, *Containment Culture: American Narratives, Postmodernism, and the Atomic Age* (Durham: Duke University Press, 1995); Arn Keeling and Robert McDonald, "The Profligate Province: Roderick Haig-Brown and the Modernizing of British Columbia," *Journal of Canadian Studies* 36, no. 3 (2001): 7–23; Catherine Cartstairs, "The Natural High? Health Food and the 1960s," paper presented at the conference "Sixties – Style and Substance," McCord Museum, Montreal, November 2003; Stephen S. Conroy, "Popular Technology and Youth Rebellion in America," *Journal of Popular Culture* 16, no. 4 (1983): 123–33; Leerom Medovoi, "Democracy, Capitalism, and American Literature: The Cold

War Construction of J.D. Salinger's Paperback Hero," in *The Other Fifties: Interrogating Mid-century American Icons*, ed. Joel Foreman, 255–87 (Urbana and Chicago: University of Illinois Press, 1997).

43 The 1965 U.S. Senate subcommittee hearings into traffic accidents, under the leadership of Senators Ribicoff and Robert Kennedy, provided a friendly context for Nader and no doubt contributed to the media's willingness to listen to him. See Mashaw and Harfst, *The Struggle for Auto Safety*.

44 Nader, *Unsafe at Any Speed*.

45 The direct reference is to William Whyte, *The Organization Man* (New York: Simon & Schuster, 1956), but the concerns about modern man were widespread in the 1950s, as noted in Michael Kimmel, *Manhood in America: A Cultural History* (New York: Free Press, 1996), chapter 7.

46 Traffic and Safety Committee annual report to the BCMA, reprinted in *British Columbia Medical Journal* 8, no. 5 (1966): 199–202.

47 Traffic and Safety Committee annual report to the BCMA, 1961–62, reprinted in *British Columbia Medical Journal* 4, no. 9 (1962); ibid., 1962–1963, in *British Columbia Medical Journal* 5, no. 9 (1963).

48 "A Word with You," editorial, *Canadian Motorist*, August–September 1965.

49 "Nader's a Nut, Says Gaglardi," *Vancouver Sun*, 8 June 1966, 13.

50 Kim Livingston notes that the city council was "dominated by members of the development, business and planning communities" and that "its essence was technocratic, corporate and paternalistic, where decisions were made by 'experts' in an undemocratic but 'objective' manner." See Kim Livingston, "Urban Social Movements: Urban Renewal and Neighbourhood Mobilization in Vancouver during the 1960s and '70s," (MA thesis, Simon Fraser University, 1999), 56. On the freeway debates, see Norbert MacDonald, *Distant Neighbours: A Comparative History of Seattle and Vancouver* (Lincoln: University of Nebraska Press, 1987), 160–2; Ken McKenzie, "Freeway Planning and Protests in Vancouver, 1954–1972" (MA thesis, Simon Fraser University, 1984).

51 One of the prominent activists, Setty Pendakur, used the term "bureaucrat" as an epithet. See V. Setty Pendakur, *Cities, Citizens, and Freeways* (Vancouver: City of Vancouver, 1972). Walter Hardwick, another of the critics of the freeway plan, made the same kind of critique. See, for example, his assessment of Vancouver's municipal governance in *Vancouver* (Don Mills: Collier-Macmillan, 1974).

52 For an insightful discussion of Jacobs's challenge to modernist urban planning, see James C. Scott, *Seeing Like a State: How Certain Schemes*

to Improve the Human Condition Have Failed (New Haven: Yale University Press, 1998), 132–46.

53 On this process more generally, see Doug Owram, *The Government Generation: Canadian Intellectuals and the State, 1900–1945* (Toronto: University of Toronto Press, 1986).

54 The transformations of the Sixties have so far only begun to be studied in Canada. A general overview focusing on, but not limited to, youth culture is Douglas Owram's *Born at the Right Time: A History of the Baby Boom Generation* (Toronto: University of Toronto Press, 1996)

6

"The Age of Aquarius": Medical Expertise and the Prevention and Control of Drug Use Undertaken by the Quebec and Ontario Governments

MARCEL MARTEL

Recreational consumption of marijuana elicited strong reactions in the Sixties. With the development of the counterculture movement, the use of pot and other illegal drugs became fashionable, as part of a new lifestyle, values, and attitudes towards society and life in general. Smoking pot was also a gesture of defiance towards drug laws, since some drugs were socially acceptable (for example, alcohol) while others, such as marijuana, were not. Public reaction arose in the Sixties out of a feeling of apprehension, because opponents to marijuana believed that its use had reached crisis proportions. Proposals for its legalization or decriminalization never gained unanimous support because police forces, some school boards, and some parents were trying to stop its recreational use, particularly by young people. These groups lobbied the federal government not to change the legal status of marijuana for fear that it would lead to the easing of the drug laws.

This essay deals with this very broad topic from a particular angle and focuses on a particular group of people. First, it examines the efforts of medical experts to define recreational marijuana consumption as a medical problem and not as evidence of moral weakness. In the debate on marijuana, some doctors attempted to define this cultural practice as a public health problem and proposed treatment, rehabilitation, and education as alternatives to the traditional solutions to the problem: repression and prison. However, this medical approach was criticized by other health professionals, who still believed that prison was a valid way to discourage the practice. In addition, some physicians considered it unhealthy for members of the medical profession to promote marijuana consumption when so much was still unknown about the drug, in particular its effects on the health of users.

Second, I focus on a particular group of people: medical experts working for the government. Medical expertise was solicited by governments to provide information on the number of drug consumers, the causes of drug consumption, and the long-term effects on health. In the debate over the different ways of discouraging the practice of marijuana consumption, doctors in favour of medicalizing the problem depended on the government to ensure that their perspective prevailed, but they ultimately failed in this aim.

My analysis of institutionalized medical expertise focuses on Ontario and Quebec, and particularly on two government bodies: Ontario's Alcoholism and Drug Addiction Research Foundation, also known as the Addiction Research Foundation (ARF), and Quebec's Office de la prévention et du traitement de l'alcoolisme et des autres toxicomanies (OPTAT).[1] These two organizations were created in different contexts and were very active because of their bureaucrats. My study gauges the influence of bureaucrats on the process of planning, developing, and implementing government policies. Studies of this question place a great deal of importance on social groups and individuals and on their strategies and alliances to influence political decision makers.[2] In addition, bureaucrats have influence, since not only do they gather information, prepare dossiers, and suggest policy orientations that reflect opinions expressed by pressure groups, but they also take into account the interests and objectives of the state and those of the political party in power.[3] In the case of Ontario and Quebec, the two government bodies saw their influence limited to simply being players in the debate on recreational marijuana use.

Why choose these two provinces? In fact, it would be more relevant to study the actions of the federal government, since it is responsible for the classification of drugs, a process that is influenced by the World Health Organization, the United Nations Commission on Narcotic Drugs, and the various international treaties to which Canada is party. My choice of the provincial governments is justified by the specifics of the debate on marijuana use in the Sixties. The provinces were part of the solutions proposed to deal with this sociocultural phenomenon. For example, in the view of the Canadian Medical Association,[4] an individual who had developed a dependence on marijuana or who consumed it occasionally should be treated rather than being found guilty and sentenced to a prison term, as prescribed in the federal narcotics law. In addition, the provinces were to develop educational strategies to demystify the phenomenon of marijuana, inform people of its effects on health, and possibly reduce the demand for it. The 1969 federal Commission of Inquiry into the Non-Medical Use of Drugs, better known as the Le Dain Commission, also targeted health and education as the best means of intervention for dealing with the non-medical use of drugs.

This essay is divided into three parts. The first deals with the two provincial bodies and in particular with the circumstances surrounding the creation of OPTAT. It next looks at the activities of the two organizations, and then it evaluates their respective capacity to influence political decision makers.

Two Bureaucratic Structures: Quebec's OPTAT and Ontario's ARF

In 1966 the Government of Quebec created OPTAT, the organization responsible for fighting and treating alcoholism and other drug addictions. OPTAT was a merger of two government bodies, the Service médical sur l'alcoolisme and the Comité d'étude et d'information sur l'alcoolisme (created in 1959 and 1961, respectively) and the Institut d'études sur l'alcoolisme and the Association des cliniques et des unités de réadaptation pour alcooliques, the latter known until 1965 as the Fondation Domremy.

The slow birth of this new government organization took place in three stages. On 1 April 1966, the four organizations were merged and André Boudreau became the director of the new body. Boudreau's appointment was no surprise, since he was familiar with the network of organizations and clinics involved in the treatment of alcoholism. The bill making the new organization official was drafted in 1966. However, the law was not passed until 1968 and was enacted only in 1970.

This slow process was a result of a debate on OPTAT's place in the Quebec bureaucracy. The 1968 law made OPTAT part of the Ministry of Health; it received funding from the private sector and from government bodies, coordinated the work of private clinics (without running them), and advised the minister of health and the government on questions concerning alcoholism and other drug addictions. However, the organization was not a foundation.[5] Faced with this reality, OPTAT officials asked the government to convert the organization into a Quebec version of ARF.[6]

For the staff of OPTAT, a foundation would have many advantages. Funding of the organization from the private sector would be greatly improved, and the possibility of receiving subsidies from the federal government undoubtedly made this proposal attractive. In 1968 ARF received more than $5 million, whereas OPTAT made do with the modest sum of $11,600. This low level of financial support is explained by the fact that the federal government defined OPTAT as a government body, which meant that it was eligible for very little federal funding.

At the heart of the debate on the creation of a foundation was the degree of autonomy OPTAT would have within the Ministry of Health. Promoters proposed an arm's-length relationship in order to guarantee its autonomy and facilitate the planning of its activities. They also argued that if it was a foundation, government action in the prevention and control of alcoholism and other drug addictions would be more credible. They pointed out that the Government of Quebec, like other provincial governments, received part of its revenue from the sale of alcohol. Proponents of the foundation were concerned that in the existing situation, with OPTAT dependent on the Ministry of Health, cynics could say that the government had an interest in encouraging people to buy alcohol in order to fill the public coffers; yet the mandate of OPTAT was to raise public awareness about the dangers of alcoholism and other drug addictions – in contradiction to making a profit from the sale of alcohol.[7]

These arguments proved to be in vain, for the government rejected the foundation idea. In the Sixties, the government was expanding rapidly, particularly in the areas of education and health. In the case of health, this expansion occurred over several years, and the conclusions of the Commission of Inquiry on Health and Social Welfare (the Castonguay-Nepveu Commission) accelerated the process, recommending the reorganization of health services through the creation of Centres locaux de services communautaires (CLSCs). This reorganization was based on the principles of rationalization and financial centralization under the Ministry of Health, which, under Premier Robert Bourassa's Liberals, became the Ministry of Social Affairs. In this context of reorganization and bureaucratization in 1975 the integration of OPTAT and the various centres for the treatment of alcoholism and other drug addictions took place.[8]

ARF was created in 1949 as an Ontario government research and educational organization, directed by David H. Archibald. Its mandate was to study alcoholism and, after 1961, dependencies on other drugs. It developed treatment and rehabilitation programs for alcoholics and drug addicts, and disseminated education and prevention programs on alcoholism and drug dependency.[9] ARF believed that the government had a duty to take action on the non-medical use of drugs. Government action focused on the users, the substances used, and the social environment. Because of the nature of the federal system, the federal government acted in the first two areas, but this did not exclude action by the province with regard to users and the social environment. Thus, ARF worked to make the provincial and federal governments aware of the limits of the repressive approach and the advantages of education, treatment, and rehabilitation.

The relationship of OPTAT and ARF with their respective governments determined the scope of their activities as well as their capacity to influence the governments, as described below.

Action on Drug Use

OPTAT and ARF both viewed the non-medical use of drugs as a medical problem. Consequently, they considered that repression under the federal law on narcotics was not necessarily the best approach. As well as regarding drugs, including alcohol, as a health problem when consumed in excess or without supervision by qualified medical personnel, they also held that people's behaviour in such circumstances affected their family and social environment.[10]

Differences emerge when we compare the resources available to OPTAT and ARF. Unlike ARF, OPTAT did not run clinics for the treatment of alcoholism or other drug addictions. The dozen clinics in Quebec were run by private organizations until they were placed under the Ministry of Social Affairs in 1975.[11] By contrast, ARF was already active in the treatment of alcoholism, having opened its first clinic for the treatment of drug dependency in 1964. But ARF quickly realized that with its limited financial and human resources, it could not treat all cases, even though, by the end of the Sixties it had more than seven hundred employees and twenty-two regional offices. Hence, ARF coordinated the activities of such health resources as hospitals and psychiatric institutions. This led it to subsidize street clinics and other treatment and rehabilitation centres, such as Street Haven.[12]

In the field of research, OPTAT lacked the resources of ARF and had to compete with other services in the Ministry of Social Affairs. Consequently, it never did any biomedical research or any laboratory analysis of the illegal drugs available in Quebec. These matters were the responsibility of the ministry.[13] But that did not prevent OPTAT from carrying out research on various aspects of alcoholism and other drug addictions. It attempted to identify the number of recreational drug users. Drawing on studies by ARF, it distributed questionnaires to students to determine the nature and frequency of their drug consumption and their reasons for using drugs. Meanwhile, in its journal, entitled *Toxicomanies*, it published the results of its research, thereby providing scientific information in French on alcoholism and other drug addictions.[14]

ARF was very active in research. It supported work on the quantification of the non-medical use of drugs, which served as a model for many scientists and government organizations elsewhere in the country. In 1969 it created laboratories to test the composition of the illegal drugs that were available in Ontario. This initiative led to the dissemination of information on the drugs available in Toronto, especially their quality, in cooperation with the Toronto radio station CHUM. The organization justified this activity by arguing that it had a duty to test drugs and inform users on their levels of toxicity.[15] From 1970 to 1972, with permission from the federal Department of Health and

Welfare, ARF conducted studies on the effects on human beings of marijuana consumed in the form of cigarettes. It devoted resources to spreading the results of its research, especially through its many publications – which included the journal *Addictions* and a series of pamphlets entitled *Facts About ...* – and in June 1972 it launched a monthly publication, *The Journal*, that covered alcoholism and other drug addictions in Canada and elsewhere in the world. ARF also disseminated information through films.

Both organizations worked on prevention and education. They made education a strategic element in the overall fight against drugs. Like organizations in the other provinces, OPTAT and ARF debated the philosophy of education programs. Should such programs discourage all drug use or only the recreational kind? Should they aim to make users take greater responsibility for their consumption, or should they inform the population without making any moral judgments? These were the issues that marked the debate on marijuana use in the Sixties as pressure groups mobilized to have education programs reflect their convictions and philosophies.

OPTAT provided its answers to these questions during an awareness day on the "problem" of drugs and their consumption by young people, which it organized for Quebec police forces in December 1969. The director of the prevention department of OPTAT, Marcel Bougie, presented the philosophy of his organization in the following terms. First, OPTAT was obliged to be "objective" in its reporting on the recreational consumption of drugs. Second, it had to appeal to people's intelligence and avoid any sensationalism in its efforts to educate and disseminate information. The purpose was to enable people to take responsibility for their consumption of legal and illegal drugs. Finally, the organization stressed the fact that young people did not have a monopoly on drug use. Contrary to claims by the media and pressure groups (such as police forces, some parents, and religious groups), the consumption behaviour of adults influenced that of young people.[16]

These education and information efforts stressed the link between illegal drug use and the counterculture of the Sixties. For OPTAT, the use of these drugs was a social practice indicative of the unrest in this period. The counterculture was challenging social values, and technological change created anxiety. OPTAT personnel interpreted this cultural phenomenon and the changes accompanying it as "unhealthy" signs and, on the basis of this diagnosis, invited their "patients" – the population – to reflect on their practices concerning the use of legal and illegal drugs. It called on society to carry out an exercise of introspection to identify the causes of drug use. In this context, educational efforts were aimed at "guiding" people to understand that drugs were "for sick people" and that "people in good health had no need of them."[17] The director of the organization stated that any drug, even one taken for therapeutic purposes, was "only a palliative, a temporary aid."[18] The purpose of this educational work was to have society take responsibility regarding drug use and especially to encourage young people's development, which was supposed to take place without the need for drug consumption.[19]

OPTAT gave school personnel a major role in carrying out this ambitious program to promote awareness and responsibility. It believed that teachers would influence parents as well as young people, for it hoped that students would share the information on drugs with their parents. Teachers were thus enlisted in the fight against what OPTAT saw as a climate of panic and anxiety fuelled by ignorance. The challenge was to make people accept the idea that scientific knowledge of drugs, particularly their effects on mental and physical health, was incomplete and could quickly change as a result of new research. Teachers had to update the content of their classes to take into account the fact that the information was still partial and often contradictory, thus ruling out categorical judgments. This was quite a challenge, but OPTAT personnel hoped this approach would ensure that if young people used illegal drugs, they would do so with full knowledge of what was involved.[20]

Since 1953 ARF had been developing educational programs based on the principle of "an interest in public education, not propaganda."[21] In 1966 it began adapting the programs to include the non-medical use of drugs. The content of the information given to young people was of the utmost concern to the officials of ARF. Despite the media interest in certain drugs, young people were aware that there was much more drug abuse than was generally believed. In addition, they observed the differences in opinion among medical experts regarding the health effects on users. It was therefore important to avoid sensationalism and moralizing.[22] The challenge was to provide scientifically sound information while stating the limits of current knowledge on the effects of drugs on health. Many young people were skeptical of educational programs that were often intended to frighten rather than educate. The director, David Archibald, recognized this problem: "Today's young people do not believe dogmatic statements – especially when it is so easy to find contradictory statements that are equally dogmatic. The 'scare' technique – warning against dire consequences of drug use – is not very persuasive, since many young people are likely to know persons who have used these drugs without apparent adverse effects."[23] Archibald therefore based his educational strategy on the need to inform, and believed the credibility of his organization would win young people's trust.

The educational strategy was aimed at a variety of groups. ARF targeted young people in educational institutions and took part in the preparation of the Ministry of Education's instructional material, as well as distributing brochures, books, and films to schools and libraries. It also worked with parents, since it was considered essential to explain the phenomenon of drug use to them and to try – as OPTAT was doing – to have them take responsibility for their own drug use. ARF's main publication for parents, *Handbook for Parents about Drugs*, stressed that the effects of marijuana vary according to the physical and psychological characteristics of the user, the environment in which it is consumed, and, of course, the quantities consumed.[24] In addition, ARF participated in the training of workers in the schools.[25]

Despite the differences in their resources, both ARF and OPTAT found that their influence was limited. Since the issue of recreational marijuana consumption had given rise to substantial social mobilization on the subject, these organizations had to struggle to make their voices heard. They were faced with the challenge of gaining acceptance for the concept of medicalization as an alternative to prison when Canadian society itself was divided on the issue. The problem was how to influence the public debate when so many doctors, pharmacists, and law enforcement officials were denouncing the solution of medicalization.

The study of government policies reveals the role of bureaucracies compared with that of pressure groups and individuals with a strong interest in public affairs. As Kenneth Meier has pointed out, civil servants have a capacity to influence that is based on the accumulation of knowledge and its transmission to their ultimate superiors, the politicians who run the government. Their influence varies according to expertise and political support, but also according to the leadership and dynamism of the persons in charge of the dossiers in the bureaucracy.[26] The scientific and medical experts of OPTAT and ARF were in an enviable position, since their officials had regular access to political decision-making bodies. Their personnel could refute statements made by law enforcement agencies and other groups that favoured the repression of illegal drug use. An analysis of the activism of these two organizations makes it possible to follow the sometimes complex paths of influence of OPTAT and ARF medical experts in the service of the governments of Quebec and Ontario, respectively.

It is tempting to conclude that the officials of OPTAT had very little influence within the Quebec government, since it lost the most important battle a government agency can face – institutional survival. As already stated, OPTAT failed in its attempt to define its institutional relationship with the Ministry of Social Affairs. However, this provides an incomplete picture. OPTAT was important because of its expertise and the legitimacy that was therefore attributed to it by health professionals and specialists. OPTAT educated politicians and bureaucrats about the advantages of the medicalization approach to drug addiction. Because of the health official's aura of scientific credibility, it was relatively easy for them to get the attention of bureaucrats and politicians, whom OPTAT called on to exercise caution. In 1969 it asked these ministries to avoid declarations that would contribute to the climate of anxiety surrounding the discussion of illicit drug use.[27]

Contrary to the experience of ARF, OPTAT's expertise was not disputed, in part because the Quebec government wanted to structure the area of health by extending its control over broad areas of public health. Defining drug addiction as a public health problem suited politicians who were anxious to take part in building the Quebec state. It was, rather, in the context of ongoing jurisdictional conflict between Quebec and the federal government that OPTAT came up against the limits of its influence. In 1971, when Ottawa created its anti-drug information and education strategy, along with programs for treating drug addicts, OPTAT pressured Quebec politicians to remind their federal counterparts, as well as those in the other provinces, that education and health were areas of provincial jurisdiction. To OPTAT, if the federal government persisted in taking action in these areas, it should do so through the Canadian Foundation on Alcohol and Drug Dependencies or by working with the Interprovincial Confer- ence of Health Ministers or the provincial organizations involved in drug addiction and alcoholism.[28]

Unlike OPTAT, ARF had the advantage of substantial credibility as a health organization recognized in Canada and abroad. In addition to its connections with various Ontario ministries, it had close ties with the federal Department of Health and Welfare. Finally, it was the first World Health Organization Collaborating Centre for research and training on drug dependency.[29]

In the discussion of recreational drug use, ARF advocated neither the intensification of the punishment approach nor the legalization of marijuana. It endeavoured, rather, to measure the human, social, political, and economic consequences of the various options put for- ward by different groups. These ranged from legalization to maintain- ing the repressive approach through imprisonment and criminaliza- tion, and it was hoped that briefs and studies would be helpful in the debate, particularly to the political decision makers. ARF strove to weigh the advantages and disadvantages of different solutions. For example, it considered that the policy of repression through the law enforcement agencies and the courts was unacceptable because it made criminals of individuals who possessed marijuana. On the other hand, it was against one of the solutions proposed by young people – the legalization of marijuana – since that would lead to a substan- tial growth in the number of users and the quantities consumed, and the resulting health problems would create additional pressure on the health-care system. ARF based its observations on the consumption of alcohol, which, since becoming a socially accepted drug, had seen the number of users increase to the point where it was the drug of choice of the population. ARF also pointed out that if the federal government opted for legalization, Canada would have to withdraw from international treaties to which it had been party, since these treaties defined marijuana as an illegal drug.[30]

Did ARF choose to sit on the fence, refusing to support either legalization or repression? Its officials denied this, saying that they did not want to compromise the mission of their organization by obliging it to support one camp or the other at the risk of undermining its influence. Instead of taking sides, ARF held that it should present the facts and let people decide.[31]

While OPTAT was fighting for its institutional survival, ARF saw its educational activities challenged by the Council on Drug Abuse (CODA). Founded in 1969 by the pharmaceutical industry, CODA had the support of the Ontario business community and the police. Its approach was much less nuanced than that of ARF. Its message was that the recreational use of drugs was unhealthy and that young people should not try them. Its educational strategy targeted several groups: young people in elementary and high schools, university students, and the public at large.[32]

In addition to seeing its educational strategies challenged, ARF came up against the limits of its influence over politicians. The ministers were in a sense the ultimate arbiters, and the premier and ministers of health were not sympathetic to the cause of the legalization of marijuana. Publicly and in their correspondence, Ontario Premier John Robarts and Ministers of Health Matthew B. Dymond and Thomas Wells spoke against legalization.[33] When William Davis became premier in 1971, he had not taken a position on the legalization of marijuana or its inclusion in the Food and Drugs Act – at least, during the debates in the legislature.

On the question of relations with the federal government in the area of health, the Ontario government favoured cooperation. The defence of provincial autonomy, the argument used by the Quebec government, did not find sympathy with the Ontario government. Already in 1968, Minister Dymond recognized that the federal government was a key player, since it was responsible for the application of the Narcotic Control Act and the classification of drugs. Cooperation with the federal government was seen as desirable because of the burden on the provincial health budget of the costs of treatment for people who had developed dependencies.[34]

Conclusion

Facing the phenomenon of the recreational use of marijuana, the governments of Quebec and Ontario relied on their respective organizations for the prevention and treatment of alcoholism and other drug addictions. While OPTAT and ARF shared the same philosophy regarding drug addiction and developed programs that were often similar, particularly in the area of education, the means available to the two organizations for carrying out their mandates were different. In fact, the enormous differences in their levels of human and financial resources made ARF somewhat more successful, even though its work in education was challenged by CODA. These two organizations are representative of the efforts to propose medicalization as a solution to recreational drug use.

This essay explored the influence of civil servants within the machinery of government, and here there are significant differences. In the Quebec bureaucracy, OPTAT influenced the understanding of the non-medical consumption of drugs. Increasing government control over people who consumed legal and illegal drugs was in keeping with the objectives of the Quebec government, which wanted to expand its control over health. ARF, for its part, had considerable symbolic advantages, but its action was still disputed. Like OPTAT, it was part of a complex field, because the social phenomenon of marijuana consumption led to the mobilization of many groups, including the Canadian Medical Association, the pharmaceutical industry, police forces, university and college student associations, and the federal government.

The actions of the bureaucrats, as this study shows, were not without limits. These repositories of knowledge were acting in the public arena and were engaged in a struggle for influence. Because their option was medicalization, they were unable to gain acceptance for their point of view. Proponents of the legalization of marijuana interpreted that solution as a new form of social control at a time when they were trying to escape such control. Those who wanted to maintain repression were not very favourable to OPTAT and ARF's position, since it would mean the beginning of the end of repression. In the battle to influence the political decision makers, it is crucial to form alliances. OPTAT and especially ARF found themselves unable to find allies in government in their efforts to win acceptance for their solution. They were convinced of the superiority of their approach (as were the proponents of legalization and the proponents of repression) since it was based on science. OPTAT and ARF did not succeed, however. Their argument for medicalization in the Sixties failed, but it would eventually become a serious policy consideration.

NOTES

This article covers one aspect of my research on the consumption of marijuana and the response of social actors and governments to it. This research project is funded by a grant from the Social Sciences and Humanities Research Council of Canada.

1 Translators' note: An English name, "Office for the Prevention and Treatment of Alcoholism and Other Toxicomanias," seems to have existed but was not widely used. We retained the French name here.

2 J.W. Kingdon, *Agendas, Alternatives and Public Policies* (Boston: Little, Brown, 1984), and Vincent Lemieux, *L'étude des politiques publiques: les acteurs et leur pouvoir*, 2nd edn. (Quebec: Presses de l'Université Laval, 2002).

3 Kenneth J. Meier, *The Politics of Sin: Drugs, Alcohol, and Public Policy* (Armonk, NY: M.E. Sharpe, 1994).

4 Canadian Medical Association, *Interim Brief Submitted to the Commission of Inquiry into the Non-Medical Use of Drugs* (Ottawa: Canadian Medical Association, 1969).

5 Letter from Jean-Paul Cloutier, Minister of Health, to Claude Rioux, Deputy Minister for Legislation, Ministry of Justice, 9 September 1968, Archives nationales du Québec à Québec (ANQ-Q), E8, S2, 1960-01-580/124, file: Correspondance et autres documents, vol. 2; Observations du bureau de législation à propos d'une réunion tenue le 9 juin 1970, avec l'(OPTAT), à la demande de cet organisme, ANQ-Q, E8, S2, 190-01-580/125, file: 1970 Comité d'étude et d'information sur l'alcoolisme; letter from André Boudreau, Executive Director of OPTAT, to Jacques Brunet, Deputy Minister, Ministry of Social Affairs, 17 January 1972, ANQ-Q, E8, 1977-07-000/18, file: OPTAT 1968–73.

6 Meeting with the Hon. Mr Quenneville, Minister of State for Health, 16 July 1970, ANQ-Q, E8, S2, 190-01-580/125; letter from André Boudreau, Executive Director of OPTAT, to Claude Castonguay, Minister of Social Affairs, 21 October 1971, ANQ-Q, E8, 1977-07-000/18, file: OPTAT 1968–73.

7 *Observations sur l'Alcoholism and Drug Addiction Research Foundation of Ontario: points de vue favorables à la création d'une fondation sur l'alcoolisme au Québec*, by L. Laforest and J.M. Bernard, 7 January 1964, ANQ-Q, E8, 1984-05-001/5, file 5.1.7 (1964); letter from André Boudreau, Executive Director of OPTAT, to Jacques Brunet, Deputy Minister, Ministry of Social Affairs, 15 March 1971; letter from André Boudreau, Executive Director of OPTAT, to Claude Castonguay, Minister of Social Affairs, 21 October 1971, ANQ-Q, E8, 1977-07-000/18, file: OPTAT 1968–73; memorandum from Gérard Frigon to Julien Chouinard on the subject of OPTAT, 9 November 1971, ANQ-Q, E8, 1984-05-001/4.

8 Letter from Claude-E. Forget, Minister of Social Affairs, to OPTAT staff, 29 January 1975, ANQ-Q, E8, 84-05-001/1, file: OPTAT, Intégration au M.A.S. See also Pierre Bergeron and France Gagnon, "La prise en charge étatique de la santé au Québec: émergence et transformations" in *Le système de santé au Québec: organisations, acteurs, et enjeux*, ed. Vincent Lemieux, Pierre Bergeron, et al. (Quebec: Presses de l'Université Laval, 2003), 7–33.

9 Marcel Martel, "Que faire? Le gouvernement ontarien et la consommation des drogues à des fins récréatives, 1966–1972," *Canadian Bulletin of Medical History/Bulletin canadien d'histoire médicale* 20, no. 1 (2003): 103–20.

10 Memorandum to H. David Archibald from R.R. Robinson, 24 January 1964, Centre for Addiction and Mental Health Archives (CAMHA), ARF collection, box 58-28, Issues file; H. David Archibald, "Approach of the ARF to the Problem of Drug Dependence and Abuse," October 1968, CAMHA, ARF collection, box 64-09, Foundation – Federal Government Relations file.

11 Letter from André Boudreau, Executive Director of OPTAT, to Jacques Brunet, Deputy Minister, Ministry of Social Affairs, 12 May 1971, ANQ-Q, E8, 1977-07-000/18, file: OPTAT 1968–73.

12 October Draft, 1968 Constitutional Summary of the ARF, in CAMHA, ARF collection, box 59-02, Policies file.

13 Letter from André Boudreau, Executive Director of OPTAT, to Jacques Brunet, Deputy Minister, Ministry of Social Affairs, 12 May 1971, ANQ-Q, E8, 1977-07-000/18, file: OPTAT 1968–73.

14 *Toxicomanies* 1, no. 1 (1968): 1.

15 H. David Archibald, *The Addiction Research Foundation: A Voyage of Discovery*, ed. Barbara Fulton (Toronto: Addiction Research Foundation, 1990), 88, 91–3.

16 Marcel Bougie, "Méthodologie et principes de base de la prévention," *Information sur l'alcoolisme et les autres toxicomanies* 5, no. 5 (1968): 7–9; André Boudreau, "Les toxicomanies: causes et prévention," *Information sur l'alcoolisme et les autres toxicomanies* 5, no. 6 (1969): 3–6; Association des chefs de police et pompiers de la Province de Québec, *Police-Jeunesse* (Montreal: Graph-O Pier, 1970), 75–6.

17 Translation. From "Quelques commentaires concernant le rapport provisoire de la Commission d'enquête sur l'usage des drogues à des fins non médicales," no date [July 1970], ANQ-Q, E8, 1984-05-001/4, file: Commission Le Dain.

18 Translation. From André Boudreau, "Le médecin face à la drogue," *Information sur l'alcoolisme et les autres toxicomanies* 7, no. 1 (1971): 5.

19 "Santé et hygiène mentale," *Information sur l'alcoolisme et les autres toxicomanies* 4, no. 4 (1968): 3–4; Boudreau, "Les toxicomanies."

20 Marcel Bougie, "Le phénomène de la drogue: occasion de réfléchir et point de départ," *Information sur l'alcoolisme et les autres toxicomanies* 4, no. 3 (1968): 6; Bougie, "Méthodologie et principes."

21 H. David Archibald, "Where We Are At ... A Time of Assessment," presentation to staff conference, Geneva Park, 1971.

22 H. David Archibald, "Approach of the ARF to the Problem of Drug Dependence and Abuse," October 1968, CAMHA, ARF collection, box 64-09, Foundation – Federal Government Relations file.

23 "Perspective on Marijuana," *Addictions* 15, no. 2 (1968): 4.

24 United Church of Canada, Board of Evangelism and Social Service, prepared in collaboration with the Addiction Research Foundation of Ontario, *Handbook for Parents about Drugs* (Toronto: Addiction Research Foundation, 1970), 14.

25 October draft, 1968 Constitutional Summary of the ARF, in CAMHA, ARF collection, box 59-02, Policies file; letter from H. David Archibald, Executive Director, ARF, to Matthew B. Dymond, Minister of Health, 2 June 1969, CAMHA, ARF collection, box 63-21, Provincial Government file: Minister of Health, 1969; Alcoholism and Drug Addiction Research Foundation, Education Division (A Review of the Education Program as of January 1967), CAMHA, ARF collection, box 59-20, Education Division file.

26 Meier, *The Politics of Sin*, 71.

27 Letter from André Boudreau, Executive Director of OPTAT, to Paul Corbeil, private secretary, minister's office, Quebec Minister of Health, 21 November 1969, ANQ-Q, E8, 1960-01-580/156, file: Septembre à Décembre 1969, Ministère de la santé nationale et du bien-être social, Ottawa.

28 Letter from André Boudreau, Executive Director, OPTAT, to Mr Graeme T. Haig, President of the Canadian Foundation on Alcoholism, 16 May 1969, CAMHA, ARF collection, box 63-21, Provincial Government, Minister of Health file, 1969; letter from Mercédès C. Gauvin, Minister for Intergovernmental Affairs, to Jean-Paul Cloutier, Minister of Health, Families and Welfare, 17 July 1969, ANQ-Q, E8, 1984-05-001/1; letter from André Boudreau, Executive Director of OPTAT, to Paul Corbeil, private secretary, minister's office, Ministry of Health, 21 November 1969, ANQ-Q, E8, 1960-01-580/156, file: Septembre à Décembre 1969, ministère de la Santé nationale et du Bien-être social.

29 Archibald, *The Addiction Research Foundation*, 145–6.

30 "Attitude of ARF towards the Legalization of Marijuana and Our Relations with the Le Dain Commission," CAMHA, ARF collection, box 58-05, Le Dain Commission, Correspondence file. See also Archibald, "A National Response to the Non-Medical Use of Drugs in Canada," speech given to the NAAAP 21st Annual Meeting, 1970, San Antonio, Texas; Archibald, "Action communautaire face à l'alcool et aux drogues," *Information sur l'alcoolisme et les autres toxicomanies* 7, no. 2 (1971): 3–8; and Archibald, "Weighing the Alternatives," speech to the Canadian Conference on Social Welfare, Quebec City, 1972.

31 Archibald, "Where We Are At."

32 Martel, "Que faire?"

33 Ontario legislature, 6 November 1969, 8091, and 28 November 1969, 9060–1. See also letters from J. Robarts, Archives of Ontario (AO), RG3-26, box 124, Alcoholism and Drug Addiction files; letters from Matthew B. Dymond, AO, RG10-1, box 35, file 35.3; letters to and from Thomas L. Wells, AO, RG10-1, file 2-9.

34 Meeting of provincial health ministers, 21–2 October 1968, ANQ-Q, E8, 1960-01-580/149, file 1968 – Septembre à Décembre inclus, Ministère de la Santé (Dossier général), Québec; memorandum to D. Archibald, Executive Director, ARF, from M.B. Dymond, Minister of Health, 27 May 1969, re Submission from the Executive Director of Alcoholism Foundation in Quebec, CAMHA, ARF collection, box 63-21, Provincial Government, Minister of Health file, 1969.

7

Canada's Foul-Weather Friend:
How the War Disguised de Gaulle's Designs

OLIVIER COURTEAUX

In his *Mémoires de guerre*, General Charles de Gaulle recalls with emotion his state visit to Ottawa in July 1944. Louis St Laurent, Canada's minister of justice, had just complimented the general, whose gracious response augured well for Franco-Canadian relations: "France is sure to find, at her side and in agreement with her, the peoples who know her well. That is to say, she will surely find Canada there first."[1] De Gaulle expressed similar enthusiasm in his memoirs for Canada's "warm welcome" during his second state visit in August 1945. He heaped boundless praise on his host, the Liberal prime minister, William Lyon Mackenzie King, for maintaining "a resolutely Canadian foreign policy" during the Second World War, and he revelled in the strength of the Franco-Canadian war alliance. "As for us, the two wars show us the value of our alliance. Doubtlessly we will, in peacetime, continue to benefit from it."[2]

By 1967 the tone had changed radically. But so had the Canadian political landscape! As the 1960s wore on, Quebec's repeated demand for a renewed Canadian federation were starting to make the federal government nervous. Premier Daniel Johnson was calling for fundamental changes, including the right for Quebec to have a say in all matters of external policy. As early as 1965, Quebec minister of education, Paul Gérin-Lajoie, had implied that federal powers in foreign affairs were divisible into federal and provincial jurisdictions and that the province had the right to represent itself abroad. Most had shrugged off the remark, but it had been enough to worry the Department of External Affairs in Ottawa. Paul Martin, the minister of external affairs, felt it necessary to issue a statement reminding everyone that federal control over foreign relations remained supreme.

By "abroad," Quebec leaders meant France. For the past two hundred years, the former mother country had not been in the least interested in Quebec. The French diplomatic representation in Canada had consistently refused to intervene in the growing constitutional struggle between Quebec City and Ottawa. But with Charles de Gaulle back in power, things had quickly changed. France was ready to listen. In 1961 Premier Jean Lesage went to Paris to open a *délégation générale.* He was received with pomp and circumstance by the French government: "[His] government and the one in Paris are settling between them, and without any intermediary, the beginning of the assistance that France is henceforth to devote to the French in Canada."

The Franco-Canadian friendship, so unambiguously championed by de Gaulle in 1945, was a faint memory. Accepting Prime Minister Lester Pearson's invitation to visit Expo '67 in Montreal, the general, now president of the French Republic, made no secret of his intention "to make waves."[3] A few months earlier, he had clearly declared to several members of his inner circle that he would not officially congratulate Canada on its centennial: "We need not celebrate the creation of a state founded on our historic defeat, and on the assimilation of a part of the French people into a British structure. Besides, this structure has become quite precarious."[4] This sentiment snowballed into his famous cry of "Vive le Québec libre!" – thrown like a gauntlet from the balcony of Montreal City Hall.

Scholars have debated since 1967 whether de Gaulle's moment on the balcony was improvised or premeditated. Certainly, the Montreal speech was in line with an aggressive stance that de Gaulle had assumed since the beginning of the Sixties – that the Canadian federation was nothing more than an artificial construction, bound to collapse, and Quebec independence must be hastened at all cost: "In fact, French Canada will necessarily become a state, and we must act from this viewpoint."[5]

De Gaulle's two visits, twenty-two years apart, encompassed diametrically opposed visions of Canada. What could explain his open embrace of Quebec sovereignty in 1967? Was his resolutely anti-Canadian stance of the Sixties a real turning point? Or was it a return to form, completely in line with long-established convictions? And in the end, what did it matter for Quebec?

Without historical context, one cannot appreciate the significance of the 1945 visit and de Gaulle's endorsement of a united Canada. It was a time of glorious victory, capping a five-year fight to reclaim France's honour. The rebel of 1940, the one man who had said no to defeat, was finally at the helm of a liberated country. De Gaulle's objectives were twofold: to reignite an economic engine that had sputtered amid the ravages of war and German occupation, and to reinstate France on the world stage. This was his obsession.

During his visit of July 1944, the general clearly indicated to Mackenzie King "that France could not possibly accept a European peace plan devised by the great powers without French participation."[6] Unfortunately, de Gaulle's power to intervene remained limited. Although he spoke forcefully for France's priorities, hard-pressed foreign governments and military leaders measured his clout in troops and hardware, not in grand words.

Furthermore, the Big Three powers – Great Britain, the United States, and the Soviet Union – were adamant in their refusal to recognize the French provisional government, as if France had irrevocably lost its rank among the great powers. Canada was virtually alone among the Allies in supporting de Gaulle's position, believing that France had to reclaim its international prominence for the sake of stability in postwar Europe.

There was nothing novel in this stance for Canada, which had already played a decisive role in 1943 when the Allies were debating whether to recognize de Gaulle's Comité de la libération nationale in the immediate aftermath of the Allied landing in North Africa. De Gaulle appreciated the pressure that Ottawa brought to bear on the British Foreign Office to end the diplomatic deadlock. Ottawa pleaded de Gaulle's case again on the sensitive issue of determining Germany's future, insisting to London as early as the spring of 1944 that France must be at the table.

As de Gaulle enjoyed all the pomp and circumstance that Canada accorded to a visiting head of state, he still had fresh memories of a Canadian federation willing to support him, despite its own growing difficulties, both domestic and international. Until November 1942, Canada had at least nominally maintained diplomatic relations with the pro-German Vichy regime, a contradictory and perilous position, even though it harboured no sympathy for Maréchal Pétain and his cronies. "It is a complete surrender ... Pétain and his colleagues are fascists,"[7] cried Mackenzie King privately when he learned of the Franco-German armistice, signed in June 1940. But in those dark hours, Canada had to consider its two principal allies. Of chief importance was Great Britain, which lobbied Ottawa to maintain its ties to Vichy. Then came the United States, which wanted to ensure Canada's support, however token, for its ambitious if illusory policy of pressuring Vichy. Washington believed that diplomatic engagement was the best way to deter Vichy's complete embrace of Nazi Germany.

Also, Ottawa could not ignore French Canada's ambiguous mood. A highly organized nationalist movement in Quebec posed a political threat that could not be dismissed, and since 1939 it had opposed Canada's participation in the war. The nationalists never stopped trumpeting their admiration for Pétain, whom they saw as the personification of France's Ancien Régime, conservative and clerical.

Despite the federal government's expressed wish to minimize the French debate, it gave growing aid to the Free French movement, beginning in early 1941, albeit discreetly. Such help could not be overlooked by de Gaulle at a time when American officials were maintaining a stance of implacable hostility. In 1945 de Gaulle did more than remember Canada's support; he envisioned the Canadian alliance in a very pragmatic way. On the eve of the San Francisco Conference, where the structure of the new United Nations was to be decided, France remained diplomatically isolated, needing allies to reaffirm her role in the international community. Canada's friendly attitude during the war meant France could rely on the Canadian government at the negotiating table. De Gaulle's obsession with the international rank and grandeur of France, which he maintained his entire life, constantly dictated his foreign policy choices. This is what happened in 1945 and would happen again between 1958 and 1969. But by then the balance of power had shifted.

Does this mean that de Gaulle developed an affection for French Canada only at that late date? A close reading of his *Mémoires de guerre* allows some doubt. Even though he was very grateful for Canada's warm welcome, his deep feeling for French Canada can be discerned between the lines in his recollections of the 1944–45 visits. The examples are plentiful. "First visiting the city of Quebec," he wrote, "I feel overcome by a wave of French pride, soon subsumed by another type of wave, one of inconsolable pain, both rolling from the depths of History."[8]

History – History with a capital H! – was de Gaulle's passion, dating back to his youth and largely influenced by his father, a professor in the public school system in Paris. "My father," de Gaulle recalls with great emotion, "a man of intellect, culture and tradition, was infused with the idea of French dignity. It was through his help that I discovered History."[9] He always wrote the word "History" with a capital H, as if to underscore its vital place in his life. In the case of French Canada's history, de Gaulle's views were already evident in 1944 and 1945. Alluding to Mackenzie King's political role during the war, he wrote with great perception: "That Canada followed him during the war is even more impressive since it is made up of two co-existing but separate peoples."[10] His words closely recall those of Wilfrid Laurier, who in 1909 said, "We are divided into provinces, we are divided into races, and that is the departure point from which the man at the helm must navigate this ship of state."[11] When de Gaulle recalled his "wave of French pride" and "unconsolable sadness," it is obvious that he was hearkening back to what is known in France as "the debt of Louis XV," namely, the French defeat of 1759 and the loss of France's colonies as set out in the 1763 Treaty of Paris.

This historical vision of French Canada manifested itself well before the war, if we are to believe the general's son, Philippe de Gaulle: "It is right to say that questions pertaining to French Canada had long since been a topic of both family discussion and scholarly discourse: I had of course heard my father's views on the subject, among others."[12]

It is no coincidence that, in 1937, Philippe de Gaulle won an academic prize for writing on the subject of Canada.[13]

These historical references, hinted at in 1945, were in plain view by 1967. The official visit of that year had been planned in minute detail, and General de Gaulle was determined to give "History" the recognition it deserved. First, there was his arrival in Quebec on a French warship, *le Colbert*. This was no random choice. The ship bore the name of the famous minister of Louis XIV whom the Sun King had entrusted with reorganizing France's colonial empire and encouraging migration to New France. De Gaulle insisted that his landing take place at l'Anse au foulon, the precise spot where the English general, James Wolfe, disembarked his troops in 1759 before attacking Quebec City. His slow progression towards Montreal followed what was once called the *Chemin du roy*, a road dating back to the time of Louis XV, which for the occasion was renamed thus. Leading up to his dramatic balcony pronouncement on 24 July 1967, de Gaulle had given the impression of having come to repair an injustice perpetrated two hundred years earlier. On that fateful day, with no restraint – his majestic airs fully deployed – he let loose his long-held feelings about French Canadians. Or, as he put it, these "French in Canada" who managed to resist English oppression.

How to explain that de Gaulle waited so long to give his pro-Quebec passions free rein? Three reasons can be advanced. First, he could not attack a close ally until the last of France's colonial empire had become independent. In 1960, on the occasion of his third official visit to Canada, Algeria was still embroiled in a war that had become unpopular among Canadians, including francophones. De Gaulle had no choice but to be cautious, and he cleverly avoided drawing attention to the "French exception" that would soon become a key tenet of his foreign policy. Therefore, his visit produced no notable incidents and, for the most part, was met with indifference.

Gradually, however, the French president's diplomatic constraints disappeared one by one. Francophone black Africa had achieved its independence by 1960, Algeria in 1962. After the Berlin crisis of 1958–63 and the Cuban missile crisis of 1962, American-Soviet relations seemed destined for a more peaceful coexistence. These developments gave de Gaulle the room he needed to realize his ambitious and long-simmering foreign policy. He had a three-pronged objective: to affirm France's national independence; to strengthen her role on the world stage, regardless of the Cold War; and to develop the "French exception."

France's national independence remained the key to de Gaulle's foreign policy framework. In his view, France needed nuclear warfare capabilities in order to join with all possible speed the exclusive club of atomic powers, to curb American influence, and to remove France from the scope of such international organizations as the United Nations. At the same time, his stated intention to defy "the American challenge" and resist the dominant Cold War template of foreign affairs justified, in de Gaulle's mind, his repeated entreaties to nationalist movements. Like a missionary, he spread his message of independence in South America (1964), Poland (1967), and of course Quebec (1967). This was a matter of the utmost urgency in de Gaulle's inner circle: helping those emerging nations to affirm themselves before being overwhelmed by American expansion (which was seen as dangerously robust) or by the Soviet Union's brutal acquisitiveness.

This was France's role in world affairs. The French exception was therefore central to all of de Gaulle's actions. Very quickly, this concept evolved far beyond its narrow goal of countering American influence and became a call for unity and cooperation among francophone nations. In 1966 de Gaulle declared to his education minister, Alain Peyrefitte, "Now that we have decolonized, our place in the world is determined by our ability to radiate, that is to say, our cultural influence. The *francophonie* one day will replace colonization ... and Quebec must be the centrepiece of the *francophonie*."[14] Those few sentences encapsulate de Gaulle's view perfectly.

With decolonization completed, de Gaulle positioned himself as the champion of oppressed peoples. From this perspective, it was inevitable that his attention would focus on Quebec, especially as he had no qualms about viewing the place of *La belle province* within Canadian Confederation as a forced colonization directly resulting from France's defeat two hundred years earlier.

The third factor explaining de Gaulle's public support of Quebec is that the evolution of France's diplomatic role coincided, after 1960, with the province's Quiet Revolution. Quebec's new Liberal government under Jean Lesage threw itself into a vast program of reforms, demanding a fundamental redefinition of Confederation that would include distinct international representation for Quebec in all areas under provincial jurisdiction. At first it was all about cultural exchanges, which in theory are of lesser political import. However, de Gaulle exploited Canada's domestic developments in the service of his aggressive agenda.

In October 1961, at the official opening of the *Délégation générale du Québec* in Paris, de Gaulle spoke in glowing terms of how the "governments in Quebec and in Paris settle between themselves and with no intermediary the early stages of the help France is giving the French in Canada."[15] This aborning francophonie – it was not officially launched until 1970 – had no political purpose, at least not on paper. Historically, French officials insist, its impetus came not from an imperious France but from African leaders who sought to fortify cultural and linguistic links with their former master. They paint a lovely image – of a France that has successfully decolonized while maintaining family ties. The reality is not nearly so rosy.

"Paris has never ceased to think of its African policy as merely an instrument in the service of its policy of power,"[16] wrote John Chipman, a specialist in the relations between France and her former African colonies. The newspaper *Le Monde* denounced the use of the French language – "this marvelous instrument found on the ruins of colonialism"[17] – for political ends, yet Paris frequently used that instrument against Canada and to promote Quebec independence.

In the Sixties, de Gaulle's long-held dreams for French Canada finally began to materialize. Several factors converged to explain why the rebel general of 1940 waited until 1961–62 to go on the offensive. France had completed her decolonization and fancied a new role: to champion the self-determination of dispossessed peoples while not interfering in the affairs of sovereign states. That was the first contradiction. De Gaulle felt he had licence to intervene so forcefully in Quebec's favour because, in his historical view, the province was a colony whose decolonization had not yet been achieved.

De Gaulle had always expressed deep regret at Louis XV's abandonment of Canada in 1763, and it was his passionate wish to correct such a great injustice. He had a tendency of referring to Quebec as "an illegitimate child whose paternity is being recognized" or as "a branch of the French family forgotten in the course of History." These expressions are no doubt poetic, but they hide two further contradictions. When referring to French Canadians, de Gaulle spoke of "the French in Canada." He did not understand that French Canada had evolved since 1763 and no longer saw itself as French. This was a long-held misconception.

As early as 1940, Quebec nationalist André Laurendeau had to be told, "The French who come to Canada and talk about France do a bad job of it. They see you as being French, and the ambiguity of the word escapes them."[18] French Canadians had ignored de Gaulle in 1940 when, in the face of Germany's successful invasion, he implored them to hold high the torch of French culture. "France is not dead" was the headline published by *Le Devoir*, as if in response. "We French-speaking Canadians are distant heirs at best, despite what has been said in generosity but too soon."[19]

Similar examples abounded. In nationalist French Canadian circles, they joked that France had to suffer a crushing defeat before someone like de Gaulle, a nonentity until that point, would take an interest in them. Also, de Gaulle did not fully understand the depth of Quebec's desire for change. He certainly overestimated the province's popular support for independence in the Sixties. He wanted to act quickly, perhaps too quickly, believing that the time was right – and that no greater opportunity lay in the future – for the creation of an independent French state in North America. Unfortunately for him, the Quebec governments of the Sixties were unwilling to travel very far down the path towards independence, even though they sought to loosen Ottawa's grip in many areas, even including international affairs.

Therefore, de Gaulle appears to have left a double-sided legacy. Incontestably, his action as a French head of state helped Quebec. Canadian federal officials had been forced to pay more heed to Quebec demands and had to compromise. That said, his miscalculations were flagrant. All through his crusade for Quebec self-determination, de Gaulle failed to understand the depth of Quebec's aspirations. The province had not, for the most part, rejected its ties to Canada, even as it sought to redefine them. The riotous public reaction to de Gaulle's visit in 1967 should not obscure the fact that his Montreal speech was greeted with much caution by Quebec officials, including the nationalists, who would never have asked for such a bold statement. By the time de Gaulle left office in April 1969, ties between France and Quebec had been fortified. Cooperation agreements had been signed, and France was ready to offer Quebec direct representation within the Francophonie, practically thumbing its diplomatic nose at the Canadian government. Of de Gaulle's 1960s diplomacy, there remained a strong image, humorously captured by French caricaturist Jacques Faizant, depicting de Gaulle's visit to Poland. To the crowd that shouted "Vive la Pologne libre," the French president answered with some embarrassment, "Shhhhh!" This is perhaps the most significant contradiction, encapsulating the entirety of de Gaulle's foreign policy: masterful in his eloquence, dreaming of power and past glories, yet at the end of the day, failure and miscalculation.

NOTES

1 Charles de Gaulle, *Mémoires de guerre: l'unité, 1942–1944* (Paris: Plon, 1959), 297.

2 Charles de Gaulle, *Mémoires de guerre: le salut, 1944–1946* (Paris: Plon, 1959), 259.

3 His exact words in French were "On va m'entendre là-bas, ça va faire des vagues," spoken to Xavier Deniau. See Philippe Rossillon, *Etudes gaulliennes* 7, no. 27–8 (1979): 82.

4 Memorandum written by General de Gaulle, 9 September 1966. See Jean Chapdelaine, *L'Action nationale*, January 1991, 98.

5 Charles de Gaulle, *Lettres, notes, et carnets, 1963* (Paris: Plon, 1986), memorandum written to Etienne Burin des Roziers, 4 September 1963, 153.

6 *Documents on Canadian External Relations* (DCER), vol. 10 (Ottawa: Department of External Affairs, 1987), memorandum, Mackenzie King to Georges Vanier, 18 July 1944, 160–1.

7 Mackenzie King Diaries, 23 June 1940, www.lac-bac.gc.ca/king/index-e.html

8 De Gaulle, *Mémoires de guerre: l'unité*, 296.

9 Charles de Gaulle, *Mémoires de guerre: l'appel, 1940–1942* (Paris: Plon, 1954), 5.

10 De Gaulle, *Mémoires de guerre: l'unité*, 296.

11 Oscar D. Skelton, *Life and Letters of Sir Wilfrid Laurier*, vol. 2 (New York: Oxford University Press, 1921), 107.

12 Anne Rouanet and Pierre Rouanet, *Les trois derniers chagrins du Général de Gaulle* (Paris: Grasset et Fasquelle, 1998), 37.

13 See ibid.: "Although Canada has been an English possession for one hundred and fifty years, in spite of this, the French language has survived. The French Canadians have remained attached to France in every way; describe and explain why this is so [translation]." (Bien que le Canada soit devenu possession anglaise depuis cent cinquante ans, malgré tout la langue française est demeurée au Canada; les Canadiens français sont restés attachés à tout ce qui touche la France; décrivez et expliquez pourquoi il est ainsi.)

14 Alain Peyrefitte, *The Trouble with France*, trans. William R. Byron (New York: Knopf, 1981), 289.

15 Charles de Gaulle, *Mémoires d'espoir: le renouveau, 1958–1962* (Paris: Plon, 1970), 282.

16 John Chipman, *French Power in Africa* (Oxford: Blackwell, 1989).

17 P.J. Franceschini, "Essor et limites de la Francophonie," *Le monde hebdomadaire*, June 1970, 6.

18 Letter from Father Doncoeur to André Laurendeau, 30 May 1940, Fonds André Laurendeau, Fondation Abbé Groulx, Montreal.

19 *Le Devoir*, 2 September 1940.

8

The Ambivalence of Architectural Culture in Quebec and Canada, 1955–1975

FRANCE VANLAETHEM

In the mid-Sixties Montreal architect André Blouin prepared to welcome colleagues from across the country to take part in the fifty-eighth annual assembly of the Royal Architectural Institute of Canada (RAIC). In the May 1965 issue of the RAIC *Journal*, he provided his colleagues with a list of sights to see in the city. He pointed out that Montreal was getting ready for Expo '67 and had "developed at a much faster rate" than he could have predicted ten years earlier, warning his compatriots that Montreal was "one huge construction site."[1] Indeed, work on the new subway system was just being completed and the Louis-Hippolyte Lafontaine bridge-tunnel and the Champlain Bridge across the St Lawrence were under construction, as well as many impressive downtown buildings: Place Bonaventure (1963–67), the Château Champlain hotel (1963–67), and a new seventeen-storey courthouse (1965–71) on the edge of the old city, a neighbourhood that had been protected by the Quebec government since 1964 as a historic district.

Place Ville Marie had caught Blouin's attention in particular. With its cruciform tower, its plaza, and its boutiques, he called this creation by New York developer William Zeckendorf the "reference springboard for the development" of the city. Phase One of the construction of this multipurpose commercial complex had begun in 1957 and was completed in 1962 under the management of the American architect Ieoh Ming Pei, in association with Montreal architects Affleck, Desbarats, Dimakopoulos, Lebensold, Michaud, Sise.[2]

It is easy to be impressed by the accelerated modernization of Montreal, whose centre was rebuilt and transportation infrastructure renewed, and by the parallel vitality of the construction sector, which since the Second World War had the support of private, local, and foreign investors, as well as increasingly interventionist governments. However, Montreal's great achievements in modernist architecture, which spread far beyond Canada's borders and regularly appeared on the front pages of the international architectural press, should not be overly glamorized.[3]

The Sixties – highlighted in Montreal by Expo '67 and the opening of Place Ville Marie, and in Toronto by the construction of the Toronto-Dominion Centre (1963–69) – seemed to be the years during which the International Style (to borrow the interpretation proposed by Harold Kalman in A History of Canadian Architecture[4]) reached full maturity. However, the Sixties were also the time when the context for the practice of architecture was profoundly transformed in Canada, resulting in a certain sense of unease among architects. The culture of architecture had become ambivalent. Forward-looking values and an emphasis on innovation, which had dominated the previous decade and a half, were now called into question; the past was once again worthy of interest. This shift is what will be stressed here; views that situate the earliest questioning of modernity in the fields of architecture and urban planning in Quebec and Canada in the 1970s will thereby be refuted. In his essay on the future of Montreal, for example, Jean-Claude Marsan views the 1972 publication of Une ville à vendre and the mobilization throughout Quebec sparked by the disgraceful 1973 demolition of the Van Horne Mansion as signs of the emergence of an alternative ideology of urban planning that focused on reappropriation, as opposed to the previously dominant ideology of growth.[5] William Bernstein and Ruth Cawker locate the first reactions to mainstream liberal architecture, so well represented by Expo '67, in early attempts at urban restoration in the 1970s in Halifax, Ottawa, Toronto, and Vancouver.[6] Kalman, privileging a stylistic rather than political reading, identifies the construction of the Bradley House (1977–79) in North Hatley, Quebec, a project by architect Peter Rose, as the first manifestation of a new architectural language, namely, postmodernism.[7]

In observing the architecture of the Sixties, the present analysis is guided by a theory outlined by architect Jean-Pierre Épron in his introduction to a 1992 multivolume anthology on architecture and urban planning.[8] This theoretical framework, developed by Épron as part of his mandate as head of the Technique et profession division of the Institut français d'architecture in Paris, makes it possible to go beyond conceptions of architecture as simply idea, ideology, or style. Instead, Épron defines architectural culture as a complex and dynamic social phenomenon intimately tied to the world of construction. It is characterized by the continual exchange of values, opinions, and ideas among the various people involved in construction: the project owner or client, the contractor, the architect, and the other building experts, as well as the user. This discussion results in a precarious consensus that is liable to be transformed by the ever-changing conditions brought about by economic and social modernization. Nevertheless, it clarifies the purpose of architecture, its rationale, its ideal, and its sphere of authority, the central issue being the shaping and ordering of the territory itself. The perpetual doctrinal debate makes it possible to adapt practices and forms to new situations, thereby supporting public policies in the area of construction and urban and regional planning and justifying criticisms when such policies become obsolete.[9]

This essay will identify the main shifts that occurred in architectural culture during the Sixties with respect to the accepted definition of architecture and its sphere of authority among Canadian, and particularly Quebec, architects. The three main Canadian architectural journals at the time will be discussed. The oldest of the three, founded in 1924, was the *Journal of the Royal Architectural Institute of Canada* (*JRAIC*), which changed its name to *Architecture Canada* in 1966. It defined itself as the leader in architectural thought in Canada.[10] *Architecture, bâtiment, construction* is a French-language journal published as of November 1945 in Montreal, and *Canadian Architect*, published in Toronto by Maclean Publications, was launched in November 1955 at a time when the construction boom left architects swamped with work.[11]

The Sixties: A Useful Historiographical Demarcation?

Before embarking on a more in-depth analysis, a preliminary question must be answered: Does the identification of the Sixties as a unique historical period have any pertinence for the history of architecture? Or, to borrow the term suggested by French historian Pierre Nora in the last volume of the ambitious collective publication, *Les lieux de mémoire*[12]: Is "that arithmetical calendar rendezvous" (as he called the unit of time derived from the centennial) anything more than a pretext for gathering the kind of media attention customarily garnered by such a commemoration? Canada's important museums of art and architecture were not wrong to organize a series of exhibits on the Sixties in 2003–05.[13] However, decades – mechanical and neutral categories that easily capture the attention of the public – rarely correspond to the periodization identified by the historiography.

Quebec did undergo a wave of major reforms when the Liberals came to power in 1960. These transformations were not unexpected; the preceding era of Premier Maurice Duplessis, termed the *Grande noirceur* (the Great Darkness), was a period of stunted cultural growth and arrested social modernization. However, this interpretation has recently come under criticism. A conference organized by Yvan Lamonde and Esther Trépanier in 1983 showed that the advent of cultural modernity in Quebec could be traced back to the twilight of the nineteenth century.[14] In his history of twentieth-century architecture in Quebec, Claude Bergeron observed the first faltering steps of modernism in the residential architecture of the 1930s, while recognizing that the full expression of architectural modernism only came between the years 1945 and 1970, a period of exceptional growth and economic prosperity.[15] Change came later in British Columbia, but the results were even more spectacular, as shown by Rhodri Liscombe in his book *The New Spirit: Modern Architecture in Vancouver, 1938–1963*.[16]

The purpose here is not to pinpoint the advent of architectural modernity in Quebec and Canada, but to examine when it began to be called into question. In the following pages, the first criticisms of modern architecture in the architectural press will be identified and their impact determined. We shall see that the Sixties were not as heroic or euphoric as general opinion – nourished by the memory of Quebec's Quiet Revolution and Expo '67 – would have it. Furthermore, the Sixties were not as vivacious and confident as the key titles in Canadian architectural history cited above suggest, and the historical significance of the Sixties covered more than that decade. Indeed, the profound changes in the conditions of Canadian architectural practice that led to exacerbated criticism of the modern movement during the 1960s actually emerged in the mid-1950s.

A Decade of Contrasts: From Hope to Doubt

The beginning and the end of the Sixties were auspicious times for architects to take stock. In October 1959 the *Canadian Architect* published an illustrated article entitled "Architecture 1945–1959: The Eleven Best Buildings since the War," which presented a selection of seminal achievements by about twenty leading Canadian architects.[17] Two years later, Toronto architect John C. Parkin, a young associate of the renowned John B. Parkin agency, gave a lecture at the annual general meeting of the Society of Architectural Historians in the United States. Parkin's talk, which was reproduced in the press shortly afterwards, traced the development of Canadian architecture province by province.[18] It demonstrated that Canadian architecture had made a clear departure from its previously traditional and imitative style, a distinction most clearly illustrated by the BC Hydro Building (Thompson Berwick Pratt, architects), which was opened in 1957 in Vancouver. It should be noted that no Quebec building was included in the honours list of *Canadian Architect* and that Parkin praised Quebec architecture primarily for its old buildings.

Ten years later, *Canadian Architect* undertook a similar study. The anniversary of Canadian Confederation in 1967, marked by numerous commemorative building projects, had injected the Sixties with great hopes – in architecture and beyond. In the November 1969 issue, Professor James Acland noted the architectural feats of each year during the Centennial decade, which suggested, according to him, a new Baroque period. He called his colleagues mad Rasputins, hoping that the following decade would be one of heightened social responsibility among architects, who would tackle the problems presented by cities.[19]

It was a time for introspection, observed the editor of *Canadian Architect*, James Murray; technology had made it possible to send men to the moon, but architects on Earth had not succeeded in solving the housing crisis.[20]

Also in 1969, *Canadian Architect* introduced a new column, in which readers were encouraged to express their views on various architectural issues. The title of this monthly series (which continued until 1978) was "Voice."[21] The July 1971 column printed the opinions of six architects on whether the Sixties had been a decade of innovation.[22] In addition to naming the most innovative achievements in terms of form, several of which were in Montreal, the respondents attempted to identify "more subtle innovations,"[23] to borrow the words of Montreal architect Ray Affleck. Affleck, considered an authority at the time, was an associate of Arcop, one of the most important agencies in Canada as a result of its involvement in the Place Ville Marie project. He pointed out certain contradictions that had emerged during the previous ten years, which necessitated a radical redefinition of architecture and its practice.

Modernity: From Assertion to the First Criticisms in the 1950s

By the end of the Sixties, Canadian architects were beginning to lose confidence in themselves in the face of widespread societal changes. This was a far cry from the professionals who, just after the war, had been enthusiastic about serving Canada and meeting the challenges of the day: the housing crisis and urban growth. Although these problems were not new, they had grown worse during the war years.

In the late 1930s, while jackboots were marching across Europe and democracy was being threatened, Humphrey Carver, an architect of English origin who had recently arrived in Canada, proposed a redefinition of the role of the architect and the purpose of architecture. Carver declared that there was no time for growing orchids – in other words, to work solely for the well-off – and that architecture must benefit the population as a whole.[24] From then on, the purpose of architecture was no longer simply aesthetic but also social, it being preferable to concentrate on housing and the suburbs. Architects, he submitted, should aim to expand their skills in community planning in order to meet the needs of concrete communities and to ensure that they shared the benefits of the area's natural resources and of technology.[25] In the 1940s, these themes were the hobby horses of the Canadian architectural press and of the profession, which, moreover, called for government intervention in the building sector.[26]

The 1950s brought a less demanding ethos to the architectural profession. The trend was now to publish articles on recent achievements in the areas of public facilities and private housing. There were more and more special issues on topics such as schools or churches. It should be noted that in the meantime, those involved in construction had to a certain extent won their case: the federal government revised the National Housing Act in 1944, established a body to support its efforts in the area of housing in 1946 (the Central Mortgage and Housing Corporation [CMHC]) and increased its intervention in the fight against slums.

In this regard, the Regent Park South project in Toronto is seminal. It was seen as "a bold beginning to the huge task of urban renewal which faces the cities of Canada in their battle against blight."[27] The overall plan was drawn up in the mid-1950s by the technical team of the CMHC, led by Ian R. Maclennan, and it included both high-rise buildings and row houses on more than nine hectares of assembled land. The project boasted a total of seven hundred and twenty-one housing units. This innovative urban morphology was repeated by the Rother/Bland/Trudeau agency in 1957 for the Habitations Jeanne-Mance in Montreal, a project that was meant to clean up ten and one-half hectares of slums near the intersection of St Catherine and St Lawrence streets. Constructed under the supervision of the firm Greenspoon Freedlander & Dunne and the architect Jacques Morin, the Habitations Jeanne-Mance comprised nearly eight hundred housing units.

But the effort was short-lived. At the end of 1954, the *Journal of the Royal Architectural Institute of Canada* (*JIRAC*) surveyed its readers. Each month its "Viewpoint" column presented the readers' opinions on various questions related to the form and practice of architecture. In addition to questions about professional training, the validity of competitions (a practice that had become common following the 1951 Massey Commission on the Arts, Letters and Sciences), and the value of the most characteristic devices of modernism (such as the curtain wall and the open plan), two related problems routinely emerged: the relationship of the architect, and the client, and the gap between their respective expectations. Among the questions raised by the editors, those that best express this uneasiness include: "Is it the architect's fault that speculative builders have such a bad influence on the urban scene?" "When a client's immediate financial interests appear to conflict with an architect's conception of town planning, what attitude should the architect adopt?" "What policy should architects adopt toward speculative builders as clients?" and "Should the architect put the public's interest before the client's interest?"[28]

Modernization and Destruction of the City

While architects had argued for a social architecture since the 1930s, at the end of the 1950s they found themselves faced with the new challenge of urban renewal. The subject was on the agenda at the fifty-first annual meeting of the RAIC held in Montreal in 1958. Urban planner Anthony Adamson spoke in praise of the aspect of urban planning that was intended to make cities beautiful again but criticized its capitalist excesses, aimed at financial rather than social benefits.[29] The executive director of the RAIC saw urban planning as a remedy for deteriorating downtown areas that were overcrowded and choked with cars. He considered it a way of creating spaces that were conducive to living and working in.[30] In theory, urban renewal combined rehabilitation and even the preservation of existing buildings, with the development of derelict or functionally obsolete areas. This method, argued Ray Moriyama in 1958, would humanize and harmonize the old Victorian cities with contemporary life.[31] But in reality, demolition was still the dominant practice.

Consequently, the importance of preserving the past once again became a key issue in architecture, but now it focused on urban architecture rather than on the mansions and farmhouses inherited from the colonial period.[32] In 1958 the *JRAIC* mobilized to save Post Office no. 7 in Toronto, a neoclassical building that had been sold and was being threatened with demolition.[33] The following year, a special committee for the preservation of historical buildings was created by the RAIC, chaired by architect Eric Arthur, who was also editor of the *JRAIC*. Its first objective was to establish a national inventory of buildings of architectural interest that were still intact or could be restored, as well as distinctive urban areas.[34]

Dissatisfied with contemporary construction, many architects were rediscovering charming old neighbourhoods, rich in visual variety and cohesiveness. In 1960 Toronto architect Irving Grossman and photographer Morley Markson collaborated to capture "The Forgotten Image" of tree-lined streets of old row houses, finding in them lessons for the present.[35] In another issue of *Canadian Architect* (this one devoted to housing), Professor John Bland reflected on the conditions that had created the attractive and rational appearance of the old villages and cities of the Atlantic Provinces, Quebec, and Ontario. Their deterioration, he wrote, was attributable to changes of scale as they related to the widespread use of the automobile – to the detriment of the pedestrian – as well as the accelerated pace of construction, its specialization and dehumanization.[36]

Quebec's Historic Monuments Act, which dates back to the 1920s, was once again revised in 1963 to make it possible to protect urban areas. The following year, Old Quebec City and Old Montreal were officially recognized as valuable, and these districts were declared historic districts. This should not be seen as a result of the writings of Jane Jacobs, whose 1961 book, *The Death and Life of Great American Cities*, castigated modernist urban planning and praised the urbanity of old neighbourhoods. In Quebec, appreciation for the historical city was not yet a synonym for the rejection of modern architecture. In a 1961 article entitled "Historic Quebec: A Case for the Conscience of the Architect," architect and urban planner Édouard Fiset explored the dilemma created by new construction in old areas and argued that contemporary buildings deserved as much respect as those of the past.[37]

Furthermore, this new interest did not constitute as great an expansion in the area of preservation as one might think; there was no fundamental departure from the values that had motivated the protection of the rural architecture of New France since the 1920s. This is evidenced by the boundaries established for the historic district of Old Montreal, which at first ended at Notre-Dame Street to the north, thereby excluding St James Street, with its banks and office buildings built in the late nineteenth and early twentieth centuries.[38] This situation permitted the construction of the new, resolutely modern courthouse in the north of the old city. Lack of interest in more recent architecture, whether monumental or vernacular, explains the destruction of many buildings and blocks of houses in the old *faubourgs* and adjacent areas, which Professor Stuart Wilson of McGill lamented in the pages of *JRAIC* in 1964.[39]

Facing Growth and the Transformation of the Construction Industry

Let us return to the debate on contemporary architecture. Although the "Viewpoint" column was discontinued, the critical torch was taken up by the younger generation. In 1961 a group of students at the McGill University School of Architecture demonstrated in the streets against the mediocrity of current architecture and reacted to their elders' lack of resolve. They submitted a brief to the academic authorities, later printed in the *JRAIC*, that proposed fine-tuning of current efforts rather than wholly new solutions. Although it was somewhat confused, this lavishly illustrated manifesto painted a comprehensive picture of the situation. It denounced the empty formalism of contemporary architecture, describing it as being motivated by the quest for personal glory or an interest in engineering.[40] Furthermore, it pointed out and illustrated new issues that architects could not afford to ignore: the worldwide population explosion, unbridled urbanization, urban congestion, the housing crisis, and the growing complexity of technological civilization.

These young people agreed in many respects with the criticisms put forward by James Murray of *Canadian Architect* in his editorials of the early Sixties. Murray also condemned contemporary architecture. In his view, it had freed itself from Mies van der Rohe, but at the same time had abdicated its responsibilities, which were not only aesthetic but also psychological, social, and economic. Urban ugliness and chaos were the proof that architects had surrendered to real estate developers. They had to refocus on their true mission: shelter, giving shape to cities, and promoting the industrialization of construction.

A new notion then appeared, that of "total environment," although it was not precisely conceptualized at the time.[41]

The architects involved in the RAIC were also conscious of the upheavals that were transforming society and their professional practice. The topics which the professional association put on the agenda at its annual meetings demonstrate this. In 1961 the questions focused on the role of the architect in a construction sector that was becoming more complex, specialized, and competitive.[42] The architect's partners – the engineer, the contractor, and the manufacturer – were invited to explain how they saw their relationships,[43] and in 1963 the members reflected on "Architecture in a Changing World." In his keynote address at this fifty-sixth general assembly, Thomas H. Crieghton, former editor of the journal *Progressive Architecture*, emphasized the changes that had occurred not only in the scale and type of buildings but also in the type of client. The client now had less control than ever before, unlike the typical patron of the Renaissance. More and more often, the architect had to report to boards of directors, shareholders, and even voters.[44]

In the ranks of the profession, however, the mood remained optimistic throughout the decade. The worries that had surfaced at the end of the 1950s had fuelled collective action, encouraged by the seemingly unlimited growth of the construction industry. This hopeful outlook paralleled that of politicians, which was nourished by the country's demographic boom and the concentration of the population in urban areas.[45] Technology and utopian visions raised new hopes: fantastic architecture was on the agenda of the assembly held in 1965, for which André Blouin appointed himself guide in the pages of the *Journal*. In Montreal, the guest of honour was the editor of the well-known French journal *L'architecture d'aujourd'hui*, André Bloc, an engineer by training and a sculptor by practice.

As Bloc remarked in his keynote speech, the notion of "fantastic architecture" touches on various facets of reality. The product of a fertile imagination, fantastic architecture can be found both in popular construction and in the works of modern and contemporary architects. For the editor of *L'architecture d'aujourd'hui*, it represented hope in the face of the mediocrity of current building, which was subject to economic limitations and regulatory constraints.[46] Expo '67 was to a certain extent a manifestation of this idea, with its artificial site in the middle of the river, its general plan based on transportation systems, and its pavilions of unconventional structures and shapes. Frei Otto, who designed one of the pavilions, was cited as an example of a fantastic architect.

To Invent the Future or Rehabilitate the Past

But the futurism of Expo '67 stood in contrast to the architecture of the new housing project which the City of Montreal had started building south of downtown in 1968. The Îlots Saint-Martin were the first phase of a huge redevelopment project in Little Burgundy. A formerly prosperous residential neighbourhood, the area was now in decline, cut off by the Grand Trunk Railway lands and suffering from its location in the southwest of the city, below the modern downtown dominated by Place Ville Marie. While the purpose of this project was similar to that of the Habitations Jeanne-Mance – to provide housing to the disadvantaged – the approach was very different. In the preliminary report made by the urban planning services of the City of Montreal, discussion of architecture was not limited to its functional, health, and technical dimensions; perceptual factors also were among the determining data in the proposed overall plan. This was in keeping with the perspective of Kevin Lynch, author of *The Image of the City* (1960), which like Jane Jacobs's book was an architectural bestseller at the time. The preservation of old buildings was also recommended.[47]

Only the first phase of this ambitious project was carried out at the time, under the direction of the architects Ouellet Reeves Alain. The Îlots Saint-Martin covered just over three hectares and included three hundred and thirteen housing units, consisting of renovated apartments as well as row houses and small apartment buildings.[48] This project was the last on such a scale in the area of social housing in Quebec. In 1971 the National Housing Act was once again revised, and measures that encouraged urban renewal were abolished in favour of the rehabilitation of existing buildings, which had gradually become the dominant approach. Beginning in 1963, *Canadian*

Architect identified the merits of this technique, far less drastic than the bulldozer method, and recommended it be applied to the old residential neighbourhoods adjacent to the downtown business district, where the buildings were worth more than the land.

The Sixties: A Brief and Superficial Golden Age of Modern Architecture

The Sixties were a decade rich in construction projects that propelled the country onto the international architectural stage. Thus began a period of questioning that was more fundamental than the one that had emerged in the second half of the 1950s. Yet the deceleration of construction activity was still not tangible, as it would be in the 1970s. Architects continued to deal with an unprecedented number of commissions. One of the architects who expressed his views in "Voice" (in *Canadian Architect*) predicted that in the next thirty years, as many buildings would have to be built in Canada as had been in the previous three centuries.[49] The tone was nevertheless changing. In addition, architects were divided in their analysis of the situation and in the future trends they saw developing. For example, it is surprising to see how two associates of Arcop – Ray Affleck and Guy Desbarats – defined the issues of the time in very different ways. Affleck emphasized three contradictions in architectural practice: the distance between the profession as defined institutionally and the new social needs; the dichotomy between the client and the user (an observation that was not new); and the gap between the doctrine of growth and the ecological crisis. In contrast, Desbarats, dean of the Faculté d'aménagement of the Université de Montréal, defended the need for architecture to redefine itself in relationship to a construction industry that had undergone substantial developments. To Affleck, who examined the issue primarily in moral, social, and especially human terms, architecture was an act of the imagination – it remained an art. For Desbarats, who adopted an economic perspective, it was a science.

In Canada at the end of the 1960s, the scientific concepts of system and environment became important in defining the complexity of architecture: a constructive system that aimed to control the processes of fabrication, and the human environment as an ecological system involving people and their space. This was a great divergence from the scientific studies published ten years earlier that had explored the relationship between people and the built environment in terms of a simple, two-variable equation (studies, it should be noted, that were criticized in the pages of the *Canadian Architect* at the beginning of the 1970s). Hans Blumenfeld, for instance, identified no less than twenty criteria for judging urban environments, ranging from perception to mobility.[50] Moshe Safdie conceived of his housing plans, including Habitat '67, as new urban units where technical systems were controlled by particular environmental requirements.[51] Michel Lincourt, the new editor-in-chief of *Architecture, bâtiments, construction* as of March 1968, appointed himself the promoter of new knowledge and a new tool, the computer, born of the information sciences and allowing for the production of the plans of huge urban megastructures.[52] If an interest in old urban neighbourhoods had emerged in Canada, this revaluing of the past coexisted with a still solid belief in the potential of science and technology.

It is important to understand these criticisms and these redefinitions of architecture that began in the Sixties as the result of the rather traumatic professional experience of architects of that decade. This era of huge projects that were innovative both formally and technically was certainly a heroic period in architectural modernity in Canada. But it was also a period – which had begun in the previous decade – during which the construction world, of which the architect was part, was undergoing profound changes. Safdie observed in "Voice" in February 1971 that the Sixties saw the emergence of powerful real estate developers, the development of a more controlling public administration, and an industrialization of the sector, something that was no longer a hope but an undeniable reality. In an article entitled "Systems: No Panacea," he asked, "Who is going to establish the standards and who is going to measure what is a good or bad environment?" He went on to say "Many of our dreams as architects and planners have been shattered over the past few years ... [the dream] that technology and industrialized building will miraculously solve all our problems ... [the dream of] suburbs ... [the dream of] new cities."[53] This is a surprising observation for an architect who had attained authority and fame during the Sixties, but it is one that is profoundly insightful.

NOTES

1 André Blouin, "Montreal ... to See or Not to See," *Journal of the Royal Architectural Institute of Canada* (JRAIC), May 1965, 48–54.

2 Place Ville Marie was part of a larger plan, which Canadian National Railways had commissioned from Zeckendorf. In order to complete a huge program of urban renewal begun in the 1910s, the company sought to build a third passenger rail terminal in the heart of the city.

3 Three examples of the many articles that appeared in the international press are "Le nouveau centre d'affaires de Montréal, Ville-Marie," *L'architecture d'aujourd'hui* 30 (June 1959): 82–3; "Ville Marie: citta nella citta," *L'architettura* 6 (June 1960): 118–19; and J.-M. Richards, "Multi-Level City: Towards a New Environment in Downtown Montreal," *Architectural Review* 142 (August 1967): 89–96.

4 While the maturity of the International Style began with the competition for the headquarters of the Ontario Association of Architects in 1950, it reach new heights with the big projects of the Sixties. See Harold Kalman, *A History of Canadian Architecture* (Toronto: Oxford University Press, 1994), 797–806.

5 Jean-Claude Marsan, *Montréal: une esquisse du futur* (Quebec: Institut québécois de recherche sur la culture, 1983), 135, 131.

6 William Bernstein and Ruth Cawker, *Contemporary Canadian Architecture: The Mainstream and Beyond* (Don Mills: Fitzhenry & Whiteside, 1982), 13–18, 55–83.

7 Kalman, *History*, 846.

8 Covering four centuries (beginning with the foundation of the *Académie d'architecture* in France in 1671), the anthology documents the changes that have taken place in architectural culture with, on the one hand, the redefinition of architectural purpose (from monuments to social housing and from the city to the region) and, on the other hand, its ideal (from beauty to functionality). See Jean-Pierre Épron, *Architecture, une anthologie*, vol. 1, *La culture architecturale* (Brussels: Mardaga, 1992); vol. 2, *Les architectes et le projet* (Brussels: Mardaga, 1992); vol. 3, *La commande en architecture* (Brussels: Mardaga, 1993).

9 Ibid., vol. 1, 17–19, 121–2.

10 Earle C. Morgan, "Editorial," *JRAIC*, December 1955, 450.

11 The latter journal is the only one of the three still being published.

12 Pierre Nora, "L'ère de la commémoration,» in *Les lieux de mémoire*, vol. 3, ed. Pierre Nora, 4687–719 (Paris: Gallimard, 1997).

13 *Village Global: les années 60*, Musée des beaux-arts de Montréal, 2 October 2003 – 7 March 2004; *Les années soixante au Canada*, Musée des beaux-arts du Canada, Ottawa, 4 February 2004 – 24 April 2005; *Les années 1960: Montréal voit grand*, Centre canadien d'architecture, Montréal, 20 October 2004 – 11 September 2005.

14 Yvan Lamonde and Esther Trépanier, *L'avènement de la modernité culturelle au Québec* (Quebec: Institut québécois de recherche sur la culture, 1986).

15 Claude Bergeron, *Architecture du Québec au XXe siècle* (Quebec: Musée de la civilisation/Méridien, 1989), 136–42.

16 Rhodri W. Liscombe, *The New Spirit: Modern Architecture in Vancouver, 1938–1963* (Vancouver & Montreal: Canadian Centre for Architecture/Douglas & McIntyre, 1997).

17 "Architecture 1945–1959: The Eleven Best Buildings since the War," *Canadian Architect*, October 1959, 52–9.

18 John C. Parkin, "Architecture since 1945," *JRAIC*, January 1962, 33–8.

19 James H. Acland, "Decade," *Canadian Architect*, November 1969, 44.

20 Ibid., 34.

21 "Voice: A Forum for Readers to Freely Express Views on All Matters Related to Architecture," *Canadian Architect*, October 1969, 61–2.

22 "Voice – The Sixties: A Decade of Innovation," *Canadian Architect*, July 1971, 47–51, 57.

23 Ibid., 20.

24 Humphrey Carver, "Orchids to the Profession," *JRAIC*, July 1937, 130–1.

25 C.D. Howe, "Community Planning in Canada," *JRAIC*, November 1946, 267; "The Community Planning Association of Canada Incorporated in October, 1946," *JRAIC*, November 1946, 268–9; John A. Russell, "Planning for the Future," *JRAIC*, June 1955, 193–6.

26 A few of these articles are Cecil S. Burgess, "Housing," *JRAIC*, October 1940, 221–7; Humphrey Carver, "The Strategy of Town-Planning," *JRAIC*, March 1941, 35–40; E.R. Arthur, "Housing," *JRAIC*, September 1942, 182–3; P.H. Desrosiers, "Il faut l'aide de l'État," *Architecture, bâtiment, construction*, July 1946, 9.

27 "Regent Park South,» *Canadian Architect*, September 1956, 21–4.

28 *JRAIC*, January 1956, 24; January 1957, 26; May 1957, 187; and June 1957, 232.

29 Anthony Adamson, "Urban Renewal and Building Team," *JRAIC*, July 1958, 284.

30 "From the Executive Director's Desk," *JRAIC*, November 1960, 495.

31 Ray Moriyama, "Urban Renewal: Planning the Neighbourhood," *JRAIC*, January 1958, 21–4; "Urban Renewal: Comprehending the City," *JRAIC*, February 1958, 57–9.

32 In 1925 the journal had begun to publish a series of articles on the old architecture of Quebec, which continued until 1939. See Ramzay Traquair, "The Old Architecture of the Province of Quebec," *JRAIC*, January–February 1925, 45–63.

33 Editorial, *JRAIC*, February 1958, 32.

34 "Progress of the RAIC Committee on the Preservation of Historic Buildings," *JRAIC*, November 1960, 495–7.

35 Irving Grossman and Morley Markson, "The Forgotten Image," *Canadian Architect*, September 1960, 64.

36 John Bland, "Housing: The Old Form," *Canadian Architect*, October 1962, 45–50.

37 Édouard Fiset, "Québec historique: un cas de conscience pour l'architecte/Historic Quebec: A Case for the Conscience of the Architect," *JRAIC*, April 1961, 37–43.

38 Alain Gelly, Louise Brunelle-Lavoie, and Cornelui Kirjan, *La passion du patrimoine: la Commission des biens culturels du Québec 1922–1994* (Sillery: Septentrion, 1995), 131.

39 Stuart Wilson, "In Memoria," *JRAIC*, August 1964, 67–71.

40 "Time for Stock-Taking," *JRAIC*, March 1960, 39–51.

41 France Vanlaethem, "De l'espace à l'environnement: la modernisation accélérée de l'enseignement à l'École d'architecture de l'Université de Montréal 1964–1972," *Trames, revue de l'aménagement (Architecture et modernité)* 15 (2004): 5–24. This article and the present text are part of a series of three complementary articles on the architecture of the Sixties in Quebec and Canada, the writing of which was motivated by a series of events. The first was the conference on "The Sixties: Style and Substance," held at the McCord Museum in 2003; the second, a meeting organized in March 2004 by the Canadian Centre for Architecture and the *Institut de recherche en histoire de l'architecture* on the theme "Les revues d'architecture dans les années 1960 et 1970"; and the third was the fortieth anniversary of the creation of the school of architecture at the Université de Montréal. The text of the second, "Les revues et le débat architectural au Canada," is included in the conference proceedings, forthcoming.

42 The theme of the fifty-fourth annual meeting, which was held in Quebec City, was "L'architecte et la collectivité du bâtiment/The Architect and the Building Community." See *JRAIC*, June 1961, 73–84.

43 Raymond Brunet, "The Architect and the Building Community. No. 1, The Contractors' Point of View," *JRAIC*, January 1961, 42–4; P.M. Butler, "No. 2, The Consulting Engineers' Point of View," February 1961, 58–63; W.N. Hall, "No. 3, The Contractors' Point of View," March 1961, 53, 54.

44 Jean Garneau, "Rapport de l'assemblée," *JRAIC*, June 1963, 62–4.

45 Philip Will, "L'architecture et la collectivité du bâtiment," *JRAIC*, June 1961, 82.

46 André Bloc, "L'architecture fantastique," *JRAIC*, July 1965, 34–45.

47 *La Petite-Bourgogne: programme de rénovation urbaine/Urban Renewal Program*. Rapport général/General Report (Montreal: Service d'urbanisme, Ville de Montréal, 1966), 73–8.

48 "Montreal: Les Îlôts Saint-Martin, La Petite Bourgogne," *Canadian Architect*, August 1971, 24–6.

49 Stig Havor, "Voice," *Canadian Architect*, November 1969, 67.

50 Hans Blumenfeld, "Criteria for Judging the Quality of the Urban Environment," *Canadian Architect*, November 1970, 49–55.

51 Moshe Safdie, "Systems," *Canadian Architect*, March 1970, 30–48.

52 Michel Lincourt, "Hellyer et nous," *Architecture, bâtiment, construction*, November 1968, 21. Published plans include "Prix Fontainebleau, Association du ciment portlant," *Architecture, bâtiment, construction*, May 1968, 23–9; Étienne Dusart, "Mode de vie expérimentale," ibid., 33–9; Étienne Dusart and Rem Koolhaas, "Prototype d'une nouveau urbsystème," ibid., November 1968, 22–7.

53 Moshe Safdie, "Voice – Systems: No Panacea," *Canadian Architect*, February 1971, 39–40, 56.

9

Art and Urban Renewal: MoMA's New City Exhibition and Halifax's Uniacke Square

KRYS VERRALL

Between the late 1950s and the 1960s all along the Trans-Canada Highway the worn-down Negro[1] towns outside every white town in Nova Scotia vanished. A sudden cut in the map and they were quickly gone. Africville, on the north end of Halifax, remains a particular and vivid instance of municipal violence.[2] On a 1969 city map, the name Africville is bracketed by Negro Point on one side and the city prison on the other. Other movements were afoot. Of Harlem, the black American poet Amiri Baraka wrote, "When we came up out of the subway, March 1965, cold and clear, Harlem all around us staring us down, we felt like pioneers of the new order."[3] His autobiography arranges episodes of his own lived transformation into stages marked by time and place. The passages of interest here chart his movement from the Beats' Greenwich Village to Harlem and the Black Arts Movement. "It was," he reflected of the move, "a socially and intellectually seismically significant development, the leaving of some of us ... from downtown and the implied and actual cutting of certain ties, and the attempt to build a black arts institution."[4] This essay opens with the artificial juxtaposition of urban-rural renewal in one country alongside black cultural activism in another. By what means can we concatenate these spatially distinct historical moments that gathered momentum along parallel timelines? And how, by that figuring, can we map art with politics or with the social world? This essay is two stories about how transnational discourses stitched these spheres together in specific ways.

My focus is two Sixties urban development projects: "The New City: Architecture and Urban Renewal" exhibition at the Museum of Modern Art (MoMA) in New York in 1967, which displayed four urban planning projects commissioned by the museum from four university architecture faculties; and a full presentation of the proposed Uniacke Square public housing development, which appeared in June 1964 in the *Halifax Mail-Star*. Both of these projects, one in New York and the other in Halifax, promised to remake, renew, and reimagine ill-used and blighted areas of the urban landscape. Through them and the discourses that surrounded them, we can see intersections in the international avant-garde and the civil rights and anti-poverty movements. These movements generated transnational discourses that circulated beyond geopolitical boundaries. Although their autobiographies centre most visibly on the American stage, they had scattered counterparts in Canada.

As an art and cultural critic, I have been thinking for some time about connections between two great movements of the period: the civil rights movement, with its nationalist and liberation strands, and the international avant-garde. Events critical to both movements unfolded at the same time and often in the same place. New York was an international art centre, and Harlem the recognized cultural capital of black America. Similarly, Halifax was one of the key places in Canada where both movements had significant impact. In the mid-1960s, the Nova Scotia College of Art (later the Nova Scotia College of Art and Design, or NSCAD) emerged as a centre of national and international experimental art. In light of the high profile of the southern U.S. civil rights movement, Halifax, with its visible black population, was redrawn as Canada's black belt, albeit smaller in size and lesser in perceived racism than the American variation. Conventional histories of these events are often circumscribed by fine arts on one hand and (black studies as multidisciplinary) social science on the other. Consequently, they rarely intruded into one another's autobiographies. Even in the mid-1960s, it was impossible to consider the spatial closeness of activist and art centres as a real connection.

Yet in Halifax the physical distance between them could be measured by a few city blocks, and in New York, as Baraka symbolically demonstrated, by a swift subway ride.

My goal here is to use the two urban planning projects to develop some conceptual strategies for reading these two pasts together. In this task, two theoretical arguments will prove useful. The first assumes Michel Foucault's notion of the heterotopia, the discrete yet multiply interconnected site.[5] The second works with discourse as instrumental, in so far as it is productive of knowledge and practices across a range of disciplinary, national, and institutional locations.

The Avant-Garde and Civil Rights Movements

One avant-garde example of the Sixties moment was conceptual art. Lucy Lippard's *Six Years: The Deconstruction of the Art Object from 1966 to 1972* gives a chronological account of random yet similar art events that erupted simultaneously in such geographically distant locations as Australia, Latin America, and New York.[6] Her extensive writings on the emergent conceptual art movement enshrine much of the work and artists into an avant-garde canon that was both centred (in New York) and global. On 29 November 1969, Lippard began a lecture at NSCAD by congratulating faculty and students: "Since you've already had as guest speakers, Larry Weiner, Iain Baxter, Joseph Koseuth, Dan Graham, James Byers, and so on, you really should be more up on the kind of thing I'll be talking about than a hell of a lot of people in New York are."[7]

Lippard could produce this cutting-edge list of guest artists because, over a scant two years, NSCAD had been transformed from a regionally based art school to an important link in an increasingly transnational network. Its faculty, visiting artist programs, and exhibition, publication, and education programs had stronger links to New York than to Toronto or Montreal.[8] The legendary "glory years" began in 1967, when the college's board of directors appointed artist and teacher Gerry Neill Kennedy as president. Two points should be made. First, it is generally agreed that before Kennedy arrived, nothing of relevance to the avant-garde had ever transpired in Halifax.[9] Second, after Kennedy arrived and fired most of the teaching faculty, NSCAD's isolation from its surroundings seemed complete. To the new president, the "particulars of [geographic] place were unimportant."[10] What mattered was that within the college, the rest of the contemporary art world could be reflected.

Retrospect, however, unsettles earlier readings. Far too reflective and political to let the record stand unquestioned, Lippard explains in the introduction to the 1997 reprint of *Six Years*, "The era of Conceptual art ... was also the era of the Civil Rights Movement, Vietnam, the Women's Liberation Movement, and the counter-culture." While artists "were free to let their imaginations run rampant," with "hindsight it is clear that they could have run further."[11] Lippard recognizes that Sixties conceptual art failed in part because its history denied its major sociopolitical contexts. A challenge to the self-constructed past of the avant-garde might be to point to other emergent cultural activities that were contemporaneous with its own but beyond its spatial purview. Such a brief account might begin with Baraka and others' migration, surfacing from the subway to find Harlem staring them down. In Halifax, the diminutive scale provides fewer, more contingent alternatives to the main contemporary art story in town. Provisionally, one could look at the music and performance work gathering around the social activist goals of the Nova Scotia Project's (NSP) Kwacha House, largely under the inspiration of Walter Borden.[12]

Probably the most common understanding of the American civil rights movement is the historic struggle of American citizens of African descent to claim rights promised by the Emancipation Proclamation in 1863. After the Second World War the political gains of the movement accelerated. Change is evident, for instance, in Supreme Court rulings against segregated schooling (1954 and 1955) and segregated buses (1956). One of the more radical of the southern U.S. civil rights organizations was the Student Nonviolent Coordinating Committee (SNCC). Formed at the student lunch-counter sit-ins in 1960, by the mid-1960s SNCC had become "a community for a small but growing number of idealistic activists, whites as well as blacks, nonstudents and students, northerners and southerners" alike.[13] SNCC's aggregate reach is what made the organization so influential in Canada. One of the NSP's founding members, black activist Rocky Jones, began working with SNCC's operations in Toronto in March 1965 during the

Selma, Alabama, crisis. Inspired by SNCC's Mississippi Summer Projects, Jones and a handful of other volunteers formed the Nova Scotia Nonviolent Project (later called the Nova Scotia Project).[14]

Civil rights activists were not the only ones turning to Nova Scotia and Halifax. In Canada, the fight for civil rights was the good cause to which progressive white and black reformers rallied. The high media profile of the racial drama playing out in the southern United States produced a continentwide support network for civil rights and catapulted Canada's blacks into the dominant (white) imagination. For black Canadian observers, the American movement was a model of possibility. Intrepid white journalists searched for an equivalent homegrown black belt, and Nova Scotia, where half of the country's black population resided, was a promising candidate. Locally, Halifax served as a focal point for rural communities, and its Old Northern Suburb housed an impoverished interracial population that could also double as the city's black ghetto. It was, for instance, the area that Jones and the other NSP volunteers settled into. Suffice it to say that the violent breaching of legal segregation in the southern United States – far though it was from the Canada–U.S. border – made the "plight of the Negro" very visible to whites and blacks in Canada.

A structural similarity between racial activism and the avant-garde is that each operated within self-referential networks comprising disparate sites and peoples. Foucault called discrete sites that are complexly interconnected "heterotopias" (1986). Arguably, NSCAD, Africville, Greenwich Village, and Harlem are such places. Each had a given social function: the art college, the black community, the downtown avant-garde, and the black city within a city. Each mirrored another racially contained zone that was theoretically similar, except for this profound distinction. The sites appeared self-contained yet were multiply linked. Paradoxically, although NSCAD and the Old Northern Suburb were isolated places, they operated within international avant-garde and civil rights movement networks; they also remained connected, or so Foucault would argue, to *all* other social and cultural sites.[15] In this way, NSCAD and the Old Northern Suburb's proximity to one another is not only synchronous but also spatial. The notion of a spatial relationship draws the researcher's gaze away from histories of art and civil rights per se towards discourses about the city and its

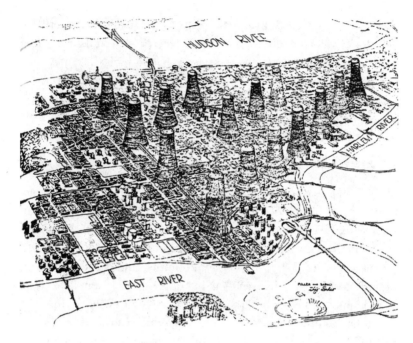

Buckminster Fuller's *Skyrise Proposal for Harlem*, rendered by Shoji Sadao, 1965. Fuller's proposal called for fifteen widely spaced towers, housing 250,000 people.

organization. The "blight" of postwar black ghettos as they pressed against white districts was precisely what urban renewal sought to manage or eliminate.[16] In this spatial contest, NSCAD and the NSP were implicated.

Few 1960s documents make the intersection of art, civil rights, and the city more visible than the 1965 architectural drawing *Skyrise Proposal for Harlem* (1965), conceived by Buckminster Fuller and rendered by Shoji Sadao. Thankfully, it was never realized. Conceptual artist Dan Graham commented on it in a 1967 review he wrote for *Arts Magazine* about a spate of recent New York architectural exhibitions. The speculative drawing produced a bird's-eye view of the neighbourhood ringed by the East and Hudson Rivers.[17] What the *Proposal* proposed was how – as if by sleight of hand – poverty would disappear by radically transforming the urban landscape.

Underpinning the drawing is the impulse and rhetoric of the anti-poverty movement (the eradication of poverty) actualized by the state and a consortium of professional "experts" as "urban renewal." In effect, this is where we see an alignment of state interest in governance with expertise such as urban planning, architecture, art, and arts administration. The government's favoured agents of social transformation were middle-class professionals, who often acted through their various institutional affiliations. As a group, they were overwhelmingly white.[18]

In Fuller's *Skyrise Proposal for Harlem* the representational scene is clear enough: the known black neighbourhood transfigured by a plethora of towering supersilos. However, its racist effect lay in fingering black communities for clearance, or for drastic renovation, and was symptomatic of larger mid-century patterns of urban administration.[19]

The relationship of Halifax to *Skyrise Proposal for Harlem* would be circumstantial except for its uncanny resonance. In the two years between the time that the drawing was first executed, exhibited, and then published (1965–67), most of Africville's homes, roads, and shops, as well as the church, disappeared into the bulldozer's maw.[20] Uniacke Square, the urban housing development built to rehouse most of Africville's displaced residents, was officially opened in 1966.

In the rest of this essay my elaboration of the New York and Halifax urban renewal projects focuses on the top-down nexus of government, with middle-class professionals and institutions, rather than the bottom-up community-organizing practised by SNCC and the NSP. In other words, my emphasis differentiates the professional and state-sanctioned governance of social ills from on-the-ground mass social movements.

Urban Renewal

In anticipation of the New York and Halifax case studies, I must situate the 1950s to mid-1960s discussion of North American urban renewal in a longer trajectory. I do this precisely because I am working against the isolated experience. In other words, both *Skyrise Proposal for Harlem* and the destruction of Africville can be read as consonant with larger processes of racialization and mass urbanization over the previous two centuries. To this end, influential theorists such as David Theo Goldberg place urban renewal within this story of modern to postmodern growth in the West.

Goldberg's argument speaks directly to the New York and Halifax cases when he suggests that "in the 1950s and 1960s, slum administration replaced colonial administration. Exclusion and exclusivity were internalized within the structures of city planning ... The 'tower of Babel' was quickly superseded by the 'tower of the housing project high rise.'"[21] The fact that Uniacke Square comprised blocks of low rises is beside the point. As we shall see, Harlem received ample servings of superblocks.

Of course, the hegemonic process that Goldberg outlines produced an abundance of very public discourse. Government agents and professionals created an ideology of invasive spatial management. On either side of the Canada–U.S. border the New York and Halifax renewal projects were highly visible. Daily print media such as the *New York Times* and *Chronicle Herald Tribune*, along with specialized arts and architectural trade journals, published photographs of models, plans, and architectural drawings. While the projects themselves produced discussion particular to their individual contexts, they were informed by an amalgam of discourses: anti-poverty, beautification, urban renewal, and civil rights.

In 1965 Canadian Prime Minister Lester Pearson followed the initiative and rhetoric of U.S. President Lyndon B. Johnson by declaring a "war on poverty."[22] The announcement dovetailed with another Pearson commitment – in his own words, the "war on ugliness,"[23] which was his creative spin on "beautification" (the American term of choice). It is worth noting that the wars on poverty and ugliness were of the same impulse. Poverty was not only a social problem but also a material one. In the language of the day, it was manifested as "blight" – poor and crumbling housing stock in "substandard" areas. To advocates of beautification and the war on ugliness, it was irredeemably unaesthetic. To this end, conferences were held, policy shaped, and campaigns initiated calling citizens and communities to action.

Like the contemporary art world and the effects of the civil rights movement, the wars against poverty and for beautification were transnational insofar as the enthusiasm for them appeared in both American and Canadian contexts over roughly the same period. The terms appear in a range of diverse documents, from exhibition reviews in Manhattan to government policy in either country. In other instances, the cross-border connection is direct, as when Robert Clack, project officer for Canada's Centennial Commission, attended the White House Conference on Natural Beauty (June 1965). Afterwards, in correspondence with R.H. Hackendahl, director of the American "National Clean-Up Paint-Up Fix-Up Bureau," Clack expressed his intention to develop a Canadian beautification program as a Centennial Year project.[24] Two years later a Nova Scotia Centennial newsletter could proudly announce: "This Province has been acknowledged as one of the outstanding provinces in Canada participating in the many CLEAN-UP, PAINT-UP, and other BEAUTIFICATION PROGRAMS."[25] However, the way in which international anti-poverty and beautification movements were taken up and made real depended on whose neighbourhood was targeted as a problem.

From the mid-1950s throughout the 1960s Harlem experienced "massive ... redevelopment that promised better housing."[26] The extent of the physical transformation was so great that by 1955 the area "had the greatest concentration of new public housing developments in the city, with 8,701 units occupied and 3,184 under construction, covering 160 acres [65 hectares] in all."[27] Two important points must be made. First, the identification of housing as a social problem produced massive levelling and rebuilding as its solution. Second, massive demolition in Harlem produced rebuilding unparalleled in any other area of the city. Harlem, it would seem, presented a constellation of unique and urgent problems not replicated in other quarters.[28]

The Olympian intentions had their Canadian equivalents. The 1966 *Journal of the Royal Architectural Institute of Canada* ran a feature issue on urban renewal in five cities. Articles included an explanation and defence of the five schemes. Associate editor A.J. Diamond claimed that the "paradox of the man-made environment of the twentieth century is that while it is an urban culture, never has there been such chaos in cities, nor such incipient decay."[29] The issue included submissions from the federal Central Mortgage and Housing Corporation (CMHC) and a preface by the minister of labour, J.R. Nicholson. Discussion of the Halifax proposal concentrated on the "central business district renewal." However, note the sly comment: "The City [of Halifax] in partnership with the Federal Government and with the approval of the Provincial Government undertook the acquisition and clearance of approximately 17 *acres* [7 hectares] *of blighted residential properties* located immediately adjacent to" the business district (emphasis added).[30] According to the journal, urban renewal in practice necessitated a balance between social obligations (planning) and market forces (free choice), weighted pragmatically, of course, towards the latter. As Diamond argued, "Public agencies [such as CMHC] may ... provide the correct climate that attracts entrepreneurial effort within welfare goals."[31]

Despite the collaboration between private and state sectors, it bears repeating that in the clearance of residential properties, the hands of government were indeed overdetermining. An abundance of very public and expert discussions, pronouncements, information, and exhortations masks the absence of the affected populations as actors. While this fact is particularly stark in Nova Scotia, input from Harlem and East Harlem residents was also negligible. At the time of "The New City" exhibition (1967), its premises and assumptions about the relationship of architecture and urban planning to social (including racial) problems were contested. Its most outspoken critic was Richard Hatch, a former SNCC activist and founder of the Architects Renewal Committee in Harlem (ARCH).[32] However, the voices of those most affected by these public debates were absent.

The Projects

My intention is to treat the two projects together so that despite their differences (and there are many), they may be usefully juxtaposed. In this way I see them as historical and material facts, just as they also figure in larger questions about the relationship of space to art and social movements.

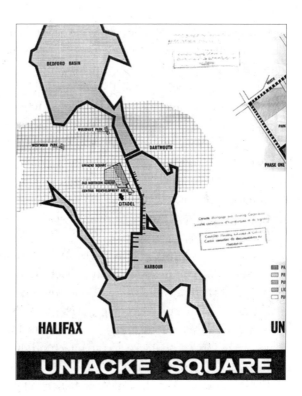

Detail, report cover, Central Mortgage and Housing Corporation, *Uniacke Square, Phase One Redevelopment, David Crinion, Chief Architect and Planner, May 1964*, © Canada Mortgage and Housing Corporation

In June 1964 the *Halifax Mail-Star* ran an extensive story on the proposed Uniacke Square public housing development and published several CMHC drawings. Situated in the Old Northern Suburb, the project would bring "modern concepts of housing" to the problem of urban poverty. The newspaper explained that the idea for redevelopment had first surfaced in 1956, when the City of Halifax commissioned an urban renewal study that would identify "blighted areas" and advise the city on developing a "program for conservation, rehabilitation and redevelopment."[33]

The first property was appropriated two years later. In 1965 the City of Halifax announced it would accelerate expropriation and would begin work on the first phase of development the following year. We have already learned of the seven hectares of residential properties. This was miniscule compared with Harlem's sixty-five hectares, but in Halifax's much smaller scale it represented an entire area. The scheme also aimed to revitalize the business district by building the Scotia Square Complex. Geographically the two areas – business and residential – touch as if at the midpoint of a figure of eight. Their public relationship was equally slim. A telegram from Minister of National Health and Welfare Allan J. MacEachen to Halifax Mayor Charles E. Vaughan in June 1966 observed that in this Centennial Year, this "magnificent undertaking" would "rejuvenate the heart of one of Canada's great cities."[34] Both Scotia Square and Uniacke Square were officially opened in 1966. Their creation coincided with the destruction of Africville, with Uniacke Square becoming home for many relocated families.

In 1967 the Museum of Modern Art, in partnership with the City of New York, commissioned four projects from the architecture faculties of Cornell, Columbia, and Princeton universities and the Massachusetts Institute of Technology (MIT). "The New City: Architecture and Urban Renewal" exhibition, which ran from January to March 1967, comprised photographs, architectural drawings, and models of the proposed schemes. The show was the first ever to be co-sponsored by the museum and the city. The collaboration was reflected in the exhibition catalogue's mix of civic and aesthetic preoccupations. Each team tackled a problem specific to a given area and presented its solution as a question ("How would we ...?"). The exhibit thus presented architectural and design solutions to the questions posed, and it "represented the first large-scale architectural plan ever prepared for Harlem as a whole."[35] Since the scale of redevelopment in Harlem from the mid-fifties onwards has been massive, the show's ambition was indeed substantial.

The questions appear innocuous enough. Take Columbia University's as an example: "How can we provide housing and other kinds of renewal without relocating the people for whom such improvements are intended, and at the same time convert neighborhood blights into acceptable components of the visual scene?"[36] Innocuous as it may be, nonetheless the question contains "the people" as object and neighbourhoods viewed at a distance (the "visual scene") and not *lived*. To differentiate the implied subject, consider in contrast Baraka's street level description: "One of our first official [Black Arts] actions was a

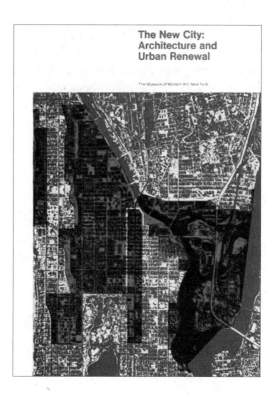

The New City:
Architecture and
Urban Renewal

The Museum of Modern Art, New York

Catalogue cover,
Museum of Modern
Art, *The New City:
Architecture and Urban
Renewal*, 1967

parade across 125th Street. With Sun Ra and his Myth-Science Arkes-
tra leading it ... we marched down the street holding William White's
newly designed Black Arts flag." Baraka's street-level description is
enhanced by information about the brownstone they burst from. The
mortgage, he tells us, "was only about $100 a month and [the build-
ing] was in generally good condition."[37] The kind of low rent community experience in this account is at odds with "the people" and the
"visual scene" envisioned in the Columbia proposal.

More recently, architectural historians have found the New City
"out of step with the prevailing beliefs of planners and political leaders" of the day.[38] Disillusion with megaprojects of the type the exhibition represented was already emerging in mid-Sixties' planning
discourse. As Robert Fishman points out, "The problems with urban
renewal were quickly apparent – but not quickly enough to stop disastrous projects that continued through the 1960s."[39]

If the City of New York was interested in solving social ills, the Museum of Modern Art's contribution to imagining the New City ensured artistic solutions. First, each of the university faculty teams consulted with the museum in crafting the questions (problems) that they would relate to real Harlem so that their collective effort would meet "social as well as aesthetic goals."[40] Arthur Drexler, MOMA's Department of Architecture and Design director, believed that everyone had the right to live in beautiful, technologically enhanced cities and that the New City schemes realized this possibility.

But there is another art subtext alluded to twice in the catalogue, including once by Drexler. This was the belief that works of art could not remake the world. Drexler himself acknowledged that art was no "substitute for human decency" and that the "arts of architecture and design" (for they are also arts) were mere tools: "How we use them depends on what we want."[41] The director's statement closes by asking, Are the plans feasible? Yes, he believed they were, because "their cost compares favorably with a few months of modern warfare." Later in the catalogue, MIT justified its exorbitant proposal similarly: "The total cost for earth moving, changing roads, and water purification would be approximately $150,000,000 – or six days of United States expenditure in Vietnam during 1966."[42] Perhaps Drexler's intent in asserting social over military action in Vietnam can be interpreted as progressive. In retrospect, given the colossal failure of Sixties redevelopment projects, it is hard to credit this aspiration. Nonetheless, at the time, many whites saw urban renewal as a progressive force.

In thinking about the Halifax and New York instances of Sixties urban dreaming, I am struck by the differences between the two projects, but it is their similarities that are most compelling. First, let us dispense with what is incommensurate. In brief, we see differences in actualization (one was theoretical, the other not); in scale (Harlem's 65 hectares compared with the Old Northern Suburb's seven); in location (centre vs. regional periphery), in the expression of aesthetic concerns; and in the quantity and nature of critical public discussion. This noted, my interest lies with their similarities.

With Uniacke Square in Halifax (1964–66) and "The New City" exhibition in New York (1967) we have two cities, two countries, and shared ideological assumptions. Regardless of questionable, even disastrous, long-term effects in their planning stages, they professed a utopian gloss. The social would be positively transformed by human intelligence combined with technology. It is this vision shared over space and translated into specific local instances that permits the most compelling comparison. Below I briefly elaborate four points: their collaborative nature, the eradication of poverty as legitimization, demolition, and professionalism.

Both Uniacke Square and "The New City" exhibition were actualized as collaborations with and sponsorships by government. The Halifax project involved municipal, provincial, and federal governments in collaboration with private development; the federal CMHC provided the architectural and design plans. The New York project was an unprecedented collaboration between an avant-garde institution and the City of New York

Both Uniacke Square and "The New City" exhibition worked on the premise that poverty was an urgent but fixable problem. Political scientist and activist Michael Harrington's explanation for the July 1964 Harlem riot was that "insane social conditions would goad people to desperate actions."[43] Interracial activists Rocky Jones and Dave Tarlow of the NSP listed as severe the "well-known problems in housing ... now critical sanitary conditions, the fire hazard effects of wood frame houses being joined together and being heated by oil burners, and the overcrowded conditions."[44] That poverty was real and pressing is not debatable. What is at issue is the designation of "slum clearance" and resident relocation as projects, on the conviction that wretchedness should be replaced by "modern concepts of housing."[45] Buckminster Fuller's impossible "supertowers" pressed the imaginative possibilities of technology to the limit, while in a similar vein Drexler aspired "to solve the pressing social problems of the day so that everyone will have the means and the right to live in cities as comfortable and beautiful as the fantastic resources of technology can make them."[46]

To envision clearance and development as solutions required demolition and rebuilding. The preponderance of disease metaphors ("blight") in urban planning discourse from the late nineteenth century into the twentieth rationalized surgery-as-treatment. Accordingly, the triadic Halifax scheme – the Old Northern Suburb, the adjacent business district, and marginal Africville – were all transfigured.[47] The fate of the business district is not my immediate concern. Africville disappeared, and only the Old Northern Suburb was rebuilt as Uniacke Square. While the redevelopment proposal called for the "preservation of buildings with historical and architectural value," the two targeted residential areas obviously had little of value for the planners, since they were completely destroyed.

The four commissioned New York architectural projects varied in their use of demolition; John Bailey's March 1967 review in *Arts Magazine* was subtitled "Destroy Harlem to Save the City?"[48] The Cornell team was the biggest offender. Its design problem was "How can we modify the existing grid plan to improve circulation, encourage development of parks and new neighborhoods, and clarify the order of the terrain itself?" It accomplished its goal by "removing half the present residents."[49] Critics found MIT's proposal the least destructive, since it called for the creation of landfill sites in the East River for proposed new housing and parkland. Bailey questioned "The New City's" racialized underpinnings. In his view, the show was "provocative only because" all the problems the architectural teams tackled happened to be in black America's cultural capital. Further, he noted that the word "Harlem" was avoided in the museum's description of the area.[50] As with the Halifax project, the racial profile of plans was submerged beneath the buoyant rhetoric of urban transformation to end poverty.

All along, I have been alluding to the racial dimension of Sixties urban renewal. The "war on poverty" combined with beautification to call on white citizens and businesses to preserve and beautify by picking up litter, planting shrubs, flooding public buildings with electric lights at night, and eradicating poverty, along with its unspoken but always implied racial face. The targeted problems in both Halifax and New York were established black communities. Identification lies in the very names of the places: famously with Harlem, and descriptively with Africville. Both Africville and the Old Northern Suburb were known locally as predominantly black neighbourhoods. In the mixed-race Old Northern Suburb, the NSP group found that the liveliest spots were the "Negro church" and "Negro owned nightclub."[51] Consequently, Sixties urban renewal was a quixotic mix, laden with disease metaphors and a racial subtext of management and containment. My final point of comparison is that the chronology of renewal reads as a choreographed performance by various professionals. Jennifer Nelson, who has done important analyses of the Africville clearance, refers to these experts as "whites in positions of authority."[52] Both projects brought an array of middle-class professionals to the fore. Sociologists, social workers, architects, designers, public administrators, city planners, public health workers, and community organizers lent their collective expertise to identifying the urban problem and its solutions. When Arthur Drexler urges that when it comes to solving urban problems, "we should want to know first of all what architects and planners think can be done,"[53] he argues for the legitimacy of these professions as much as for the housing needs of marginalized sectors. In closing, one might ask how the Nova Scotia College of Art and Design (NSCAD) figures in the urban renewal project. While "The New City" exhibition explicitly makes the connection between contemporary art and urban planning, in Halifax there was no clear connection between the renewal projects and the only recognized locus of experimental art activity in the city. However, there were indirect connections if framed in terms of spatial organization. Suffice to say, the college in those days was a considerable distance from both of the targeted residential sites and was well within the city's white district.

Involvement with municipal beautification and redevelopment is part of NSCAD's history. Between 1967 and 1968 the college completed a six-storey addition. In 1979 it relocated to the historic waterfront properties, thus extending the business district that had been redeveloped by the Scotia Square Complex more than a decade earlier. On the occasion of NSCAD's opening in the waterfront properties, College President Kennedy noted, "Our decision to relocate has been ... vital ... in preserving a most important section of historic Halifax." The statement aligns the college's position with the part of the city possessing historic value and with the business sector.

To further emphasize NSCAD's position within the redevelopment scheme, let me contrast it briefly with the fate of the NSP. Whereas the college was the acknowledged centre of contemporary and experimental art, the NSP was barely visible as an organization and cultural centre. Although the NSP was at the centre of opposition to the Uniacke Square development, it infused drama, music, and dance into its activities. Where NSCAD expanded, the NSP between the summer of 1965 and the fall of 1968 struggled through three different locations around the circumference of the Old Northern Suburb. Its last location was demolished to make way for an Olympic-sized swimming pool, partially funded by federal Centennial monies.

My task in looking at these two Sixties redevelopment projects, one in New York and the other in Halifax, has been to explore how transnational discourses linked the spatially segregated spheres of the avantgarde and civil rights movements. Anti-poverty movement discourses, combined with the civil rights movement's claims for equity, provided a rationale for targeting low-income black communities for clearance. By emphasizing the eradication of poverty, the projects could mask the racial effects of demolition and selective rebuilding. "The New City" exhibition foregrounds the collusion of university faculties with a major art institution and government to articulate a pervasive vision. In Halifax, the three-part plan affirms James St. George Walker's observation that "Africville has been Canada's most highly publicized black community, but it is by no means unique."[54] Legendary moments in the history of experimental art at NSCAD coincided with the building, redevelopment, and refitting of the college for a particular coterie of white art producers. Just as Lucy Lippard acknowledged, Sixties conceptual art dissociated itself from concurrent social movements that were unfolding on its own doorstep in New York. So, too, did conceptual art and civil rights activism in Halifax develop along two racially segregated trajectories.[55]

The act of making connections among these segregated, local, racial, and disciplinary accounts has been a tentative exploration. However, if we let other kinds of material evidence "speak," as I was compelled to do by Fuller's *Skyrise Proposal for Harlem*, Baraka's Blacks Arts parade across 125th Street, and the NSP's performances, then perhaps we may encounter other approaches to understanding the relationship of art to political struggle.

NOTES

1 Throughout this chapter I refer to people of African heritage as black and those of Anglo-European heritage as white. George Elliot Clarke and others have used the term Africadian to denote blacks from Nova Scotia, where the dominant white population was historically descended from Scottish settlers. Because the terms "Negro" and "coloured" currently carry aspersions, I use them only to evoke the historical moment of the early to late 1960s, when they were in common usage by both whites and blacks.

2 Other sizable black areas existed, but on the City of Halifax's immediate outskirts; Africville was the closest, at the city's northern edge. Other communities, such as Preston and Cherry Brook, were well outside city boundaries.

3 Amiri Baraka [LeRoi Jones], *The Autobiography of LeRoi Jones* (Chicago: Lawrence Hill Books, 1997), 295.

4 Ibid., 297.

5 Michel Foucault, "Of Other Spaces," *Diacritics* (1986): 22–7.

6 Lucy Lippard, *Six Years: The Dematerialization of the Art Object from 1966 to 1972* (Berkeley: University of California Press, 1997).

7 Lucy Lippard, "Toward a Dematerialized or Non Object Art," lecture given 29 November 1969 (photocopy), AV collection, Nova Scotia College of Art and Design (NSCAD) Library, Halifax.

8 Garry Neill Kennedy, "The Nova Scotia College of Art and Design and the Sixties: A Memoir," *Canadian Literature: A Quarterly of Criticism and Review*, Spring–Summer 1997, 195. The movement of students and faculty between Halifax and New York would be ensured in 1973 when NSCAD established its New York loft as a satellite site for faculty and students visiting New York. See Bruce Barber, *Conceptual Art: The NSCAD Connection, 1967–1973*, exhibition catalogue (Halifax: Anna Leonowens Gallery, 2001), 11, 15.

9 John Murchie, "On Making a Substantial Art," in *Garry Neill Kennedy: Work of Four Decades* (Halifax: Art Gallery of Nova Scotia, 2000), 150; Kennedy, "The Nova Scotia College," 192–3.

10 Robert Stacey and Liz Wylie, *Eighty/Twenty: 100 Years of the Nova Scotia College of Art and Design*, exhibition catalogue (Halifax: Art Gallery of Nova Scotia, 1988), 76.

11 Lippard, *Six Years*, vii.

12 Walter Borden, taped interview by author, Toronto, 16 February 2004, and telephone interview by author, 11 May 2003. See also Rocky Jones, "General Activities of the Past Three Months," *Nova Scotia Scene*, June 1966, 4.

13 Clayborne Carson, *In Struggle: SNCC and the Black Awakening of the 1960s* (Cambridge, Mass.: Harvard University Press, 1981), 1.

14 Interview by author with Rocky Jones, February 2003.

15 Foucault's often-quoted phrase begins: "We do not live inside a void ... we live inside a set of relations that delineates sites which are irreducible to one another" (Foucault, "Of Other Spaces," 23).

16 I turn to the growing body of critical literature on space and race to uncover the synchronicity of the two movements in a small Canadian city far removed from the places that gave them their renowned public presence. See, for example, David Theo Goldberg, "The New Segregation" and "'Polluting the Body Politic': Race and Urban Location," in *Racism, the City, and the State*, ed. Michael Keith and Malcolm Cross (London: Routledge, 1993); George Elliot Clarke, "Honouring African-Canadian Geography: Mapping the Black Presence in Atlantic Canada," *Borderlines*, December 1997, 35–9; and Rinaldo Walcott, *Black Like Who? Writing Black Canada* (Toronto: Insomniac Press, 1997). A shortcoming of my own analysis is an overprivileging of the category of race. Despite the omission, I agree with Jennifer Nelson's point that much of the theoretical literature speaks to the "interlocking dynamics of space and subject formation" which announces the "co-presence of race, gender, class and sexuality." See Nelson's "The Operation of Whiteness and Forgetting in Africville: A Geography of Racism" (PHD dissertation, University of Toronto, 2001), 27.

17 Buckminster Fuller and Shoji Sadao, *Skyrise Proposal for Harlem*, 1965. Rendering by Sadao.

18 Nelson, "The Operation of Whiteness"; Nelson, "The Space of Africville: Creating, Regulating, and Remembering the Urban Slum," *Canadian Journal of Law and Society* 15, no. 2 (2000); and Goldberg, "New Segregation" and "Polluting the Body Politic."

19 Goldberg, "Polluting the Body Politic," 49.

20 The story of Africville has been well recorded. See Clarke, "Honouring African-Canadian Geography"; James W. St. George Walker, "Allegories and Orientation in African-Canadian Historiography: The Spirit of Africville," *Dalhousie Review*, Summer 1997, 155–77; Nelson, "The Operation of Whiteness" and "The Space of Africville"; Donald H.

Clairmont and Dennis William Magill, *Africville: The Life and Death of a Canadian Black Community*, 3rd edn (Toronto: Scholars Press, 1999).

21 Goldberg, "Polluting the Body Politic," 46–7.

22 Margaret Little, "The Struggle Over the Meaning of Deserving, 1965–1995," in *No Car, No Radio, No Liquor Permit: The Moral Regulation of Single Mothers in Ontario, 1920–1997* (Toronto: Oxford University Press, 1998), 137–63. Little makes the observation that the collection "of statistical data on poverty began in the early 1960s and increased public awareness of the problem." See also Arthur Marwick, *The Sixties* (Oxford & New York: Oxford University Press, 1998), 268–71. Marwick states, "The main features of the American 'great society,' whose two keynote acts both became law in 1964, were the Civil Rights Act ... and the Economic Opportunity Act" (268).

23 Community Planning Association of Canada, "Community Planning Association: Centennial Year-National Conference," Library and Archives Canada (LAC), RG 69, vol. 518, 4.

24 R. Clack, letter to R.H. Hackendahl, 23 November 1965, TLS Collection, LAC, RG 69, vol. 518.

25 *Nova Scotia Centennial News Briefs*, October 1967, 1.

26 Robert A.M. Stern, Thomas Mellins, and David Fishman, *New York 1960: Architecture and Urbanism between the Second World War and the Bicentennial* (New York: Tashen, 1997), 858.

27 Ibid.

28 While my focus is Canada and the United States, similar initiatives were transforming other Western cities. Simon Sadler's study of the European anarchist artist group, Situationist International (1957–1972), observed that from the early 1950s to the early 1960s, the "scale of postwar redevelopment planned for Paris ... was unprecedented since Haussmann. It has been estimated that at least a third of the old Ville de Paris disappeared." See *The Situationist City* (Cambridge, Mass.: MIT Press, 1998), 58.

29 *Journal of the Royal Architectural Institute of Canada* (JRAIC), June 1966, 33.

30 Project title is "Uniacke Square: Halifax N.S. Central Business District Renewal." See *JRAIC*, June 1966, 39.

31 *JRAIC*, June 1966, 33.

32 Stern, Mellins, and Fishman, *New York 1960*, 858.

33 Mike Bembridge, "Uniacke Square Housing Plans Unveiled by CMCH: 184 Apartment Units Involved in First Phase," *Halifax Mail-Star*, 15 June 1965.

34 A.J. MacEachen, letter to C.E. Vaughan, CN Telecommunications, 21 June 1966, LAC, RG69, vol. 773.

35 Stern, Mellins, and Fishman, *New York 1960*, 859.

36 Arthur Drexler with Sidney J. Frigand and Elisabeth Kassler, eds., *The New City: Architecture and Urban Renewal: An Exhibition of the Museum of Modern Art, New York, January 23 to March 13, 1967* (New York: Museum of Modern Art, 1967), 30.

37 Baraka, *Autobiography of LeRoi Jones*, 299.

38 Stern, Mellins, and Fishman, *New York 1960*, 859.

39 Robert Fishman, ed., "The American Planning Tradition: An Introduction and Interpretation," in *The American Planning Tradition: Culture and Policy* (Washington, DC: Woodrow Centre Press, 2000), 17.

40 *The New City*, 22.

41 Ibid.

42 Ibid., 42.

43 Stern, Mellins, and Fishman, *New York 1960*, 858.

44 Nova Scotia Project (NSP), *Nova Scotia Scene*, June 1966, 4½. As noted above, the NSP was originally called the Nova Scotia Nonviolent Project. It was one of five programs initiated by a national New Left organization called the Student Union for Peace Action (SUPA). SUPA's Summer Projects of 1965, as well as the initial inclusion of "nonviolence" in NSP's name, illustrate the organization's close ties to a radical southern U.S. civil rights group, the Student Nonviolent Coordinating Committee (SNCC).

45 Bembridge, "Uniacke Square."

46 *The New City*, 22.

47 *JRAIC*, June 1966, cover.

48 John Bailey, "Chicken Little: Destroy Harlem to Save the City?" *Arts Magazine*, March 1967.

49 C. Richard Hatch, "The MOMA Discovers Harlem," *Architectural Forum*, March 1967, 42.

50 Ibid.

51 NSP, *Nova Scotia Scene*, December 1965.

52 Nelson, "The Operation of Whiteness," 2.

53 *The New City*, 22.

54 Walker, "Allegories and Orientations," 155.

55 Lippard, *Six Years*.

10

California Casual:
How the Slouch Sold the Modern

NICHOLAS OLSBERG

I could recount how I arrived in North America as a graduate student from the north of England in August 1965 by recalling that, given my late application, I had been set up in a dorm room with a flashy sophomore called Jeff. He had kept the left side of the closet free for me, and it took no more than five minutes to place in it my short and well-worn stack of navy blue serge and dark brown tweed, a pea jacket, a duffel coat, a little grey flannel, and some white cotton. Jeff drove an open steel-blue Corvette, and the right side of the closet was piled high in a gorgeous rainbow of clothing for convertibles: slacks and Bermudas sorted along the spectrum from scarlet to lime green, short-sleeve madras shirts in stripes and checks of every hue, mohair and alpaca sweaters fanatically graded, like a Benjamin Moore paint sample, into a comprehensive range of pastels. Out of the window on the lawns, a thousand young women topped with bobbed hair and grosgrain headbands sported their bright Villager blouses and Pappagallo pumps. "I love it here," my mother said when she came to visit a year later. "I never imagined students anywhere looking so fresh, clean, and hopeful." "How could they look anything else," grumbled my father, "when they are all dressed like children at a birthday party."

Or I could tell a quite different story by recalling that as I flew into Kennedy airport the day before, the plane circled an already disastrous World's Fair – organized for the twenty-fifth anniversary of the one that had announced "Tomorrow" – just as five thousand visitors celebrated the last weekend by rampaging through its visions of the next tomorrow, leaving them in ruins; that as I sat sweating in an immigration booth, ritually denying intent to subvert democracy, with the air-conditioning turned off to guard against a terrible drought, we stood about halfway between the assassinations of Jack and Malcolm and those of Bobby and Martin; and that 250 square kilometres of Los Angeles were still smoke and smoulder, following the first in an annual summer series of deadly mass assaults by the disadvantaged young against the crumbling fabric of cities across America. A few months later, three days of havoc and riot wracked the streets of Montreal when its police force went on strike; and not much more than a year after my parents' visit, I stood on another college lawn less than an hour away as three black teenagers were slaughtered in the dark by the National Guard.

The disjunction between confidence and despair – between consuming America's official products and challenging its official ideologies, between "long hot summers" and the Summer of Love – colours everything about the world that lived under the U.S. umbrella in the Sixties. Except for common origins in youth and recklessness, even the decade's revolts were inconsistent, fluctuating between the playful and the dangerous, the freethinking and the prescriptive, the ideal and the dystopic.

The assault on war began with the teach-in and ended with the Weathermen. The new democracy of community action that made a people's park in one town produced a busing crisis in another. One attack on chastity started with the love-in and quite another with Larry Flynt. The women's movement commenced with burning bras and quickly moved to putting everyday conversation into corsets. Journeys to liberate consciousness that began by squatting around Allen Ginsberg and chanting to a tambourine concluded in the drug-poisoned solitudes that silenced Janis Joplin, Jimi Hendrix, Jim Morrison, and thousands of other not so famous sons and daughters. Even, perhaps especially, when they were at their gentlest, each of these revolutions left a wave of insulted fury in its wake. Parents warred with their children over hair. "Sexist" construction crews from Queens traded whistles with "liberated" women from Manhattan. "An Okie from Muskokee" declared cultural superiority over the hippie from the Haight. These culture wars might have been about substance, but the fields of battle were taste and style.

So it is all the more remarkable that one of the most sweeping cultural changes of the time – a near-universal informalizing and infantilizing of everyday dress and the blurring of distinctions in posture, deportment, rank, and occasion that went with it – crept in quietly. Short-lived disputes over turtlenecks, miniskirts, and topless dresses were good-humoured, not just in contrast to the generally rancorous clamour of the era but in comparison to the preceding half-century of social contention over dress. Decade after decade, differing ethnicities, classes, age groups, and moral traditions had fought each other over changes in clothing, from bloomers and stockings to flappers' sheaths, from oxford bags and knickers to zoot suits, from Teddy-boy collars and bobby soxers to tight blue jeans. Only one uproar of the Sixties came close: a summer of weekend confrontations at English seaside resorts, two years into the new decade. It pitched motorbikes against Vespas, British black leather and chain against transatlantic sunglasses and coloured slacks. These engagements between Rockers and Mods were not against the young but among them. They set blue-collar tradition against petit bourgeois aspiration, blokes without girls against guys with easy ones, wintry gear against Riviera wear, Bermondsey against Basingstoke.

Mod worked worldwide, playing with differing regional dynamics to loosen the conventions and class distinctions of newly prospering leisured societies. It has persisted into an era in which nearly everything else in the streamlined, progressive, and egalitarian spirit of the modern has been discarded, leaving us to lounge around our neo-Victorian homes incongruously dressed in the vestiges of mid-twentieth-century modernity.

The idea that clothing might no longer be a social marker came from one place, Los Angeles. The city had a massive market interest in advancing it and a particular local convergence of economic forces, design aesthetics, and cultural mythologies in place to promote it. From about the time the movies arrived, right through the aerospace boom of the Cold War years, the city was built on the will to grow and, with that will, on selling the idea of a home of your own in a sunlit garden to the millions of Americans who might come west to make growth happen. As late as the year 2000, 40 percent of employment in the Los Angeles basin – property law, sales, civil engineering, architecture, design, mortgage banking, gardens, and maintenance – was still related to building, selling, or servicing real estate.

Indeed, the private dwelling was the primary engine of the region's public economy, right from the completion of the suburban rail system – a network so fast and so extensive that the landowners and bankers who built it could readily develop house lots sixty kilometres from the city's centre. As a result, new arrivals, once they got there, could commute to the city from their homes with comfort. So successful was this alliance of interests that it took only twelve years for the population to grow too fast for even the electric railway to service it and for quite another plan to emerge. This plan, not unrelated to the fact that nearly every local newspaper could now report an oil strike, strung commerce and services out along vast ribbons of roadway – roadway that touched nearly all the subdevelopments built so far and a thousand more still to be built. By the time of the 1929 crash, in a city already studded with drive-in markets, drive-up schools, country clubs, and roadside savings banks, Los Angeles already counted more cars per household than any other city in the world could in 1950.

When local car dealers opened the country's first radio stations to advertise their wares better, a league between entertainment and the great suburban plan began. The music sold the radio, the radio sold the car, the car took you to the land office, and the branch bank sold you the house. The home became a sort of gospel. The city's leading entertainer of the 1920s, the evangelist Aimee Semple McPherson, preached nightly on the miracle of being led to California to find a little home. Films now premiered miles from Hollywood in towering "landmark" cinemas that were set up to draw potential home buyers to barely built suburbs. At the same time, the cult of "stars at home" began. Tourists now spent half their time in Hollywood looking at the façades of actors' houses. Illustrated magazines that once showed a loosely attired movie idol lazing in layered chiffon on the divan of an exotic set now showed a loosely attired movie idol lazing in casual cotton on the rattan chaise longue of her patio, or one stepping out of an open roadster by the cottage door, her short car coat draped over the shoulder of her golf shirt.

The mass-market assembly-line automobile was developed in the traditional streetcar cities of the East just as the boom following the First World War began, as much for recreation as convenience, more to escape the city than to function efficiently within it. Hence, the car was already associated with leisure and with leisured dress. But it had a small gas tank, used fuel rapidly, needed air and water frequently, took time to start, and – in Los Angeles – ran on hot, rough, and dusty roads. On the way home, men turned off the highway only once – at a service station next to a flower shop next to a drugstore. Women, however, often bought groceries, filled the car, played a game of tennis, had lunch at the drugstore, and kept an appointment with the hairdresser, all as part of the same foray. This left them with little time to change clothes.

It was quickly apparent that traditional street clothes served the circumstances ill. The first drive-in markets were designed so that middle-class housewives could order from the car, in curlers if they chose, and have their groceries brought to them. Hard on the heels of these drive-ins came the housecoat, the car coat, and the flat pump. The car, for such women, was fast becoming an extension of the home, and moving to and from it, or in and out of it, the most frequent occasion for a public appearance. For working-class families in a city without public parks, the weekend drive – ending at some form of communal parking, whether the food stand on the beach, an airfield event, a land promotion, or a picnic grove – was the principal recreational and social activity. Leisure and movement, private comfort and public display now went hand in hand, and distinctions between street dress and house clothes, indoors and out, began to seem senseless.

It was in this emerging culture of mobility that southern California's clothing industry first took off. As the city's wave of middle-income immigration tailed off in the 1930s, equally potent waves of new mythmaking and stylistic innovation kept the market for new housing alive. As the new city sought new ways to configure its supposed history and possible future, the wooden cottage of the 1910s was replaced by the Spanish stucco house of the 1920s. Then came the brick, wood, and windows of the simpler Monterey and Regency styles. In turn, these were replaced by a "modern look." For this, the mortgage banks hired architects to find a domestic aesthetic to match the spirit of speed seen in the streamlining of the car and the sheen of the DC 2, in the open aisles, slick counters, and aluminum stools of the first great drugstores and supermarkets, and in the tubular steel, curved lines, and mirrored walls of the movie sets which European designers introduced to Hollywood as soon as lights and microphones could be strung up on booms to allow the now talking actors to move around.

Just as the car had erased the distinction between dressing for street and dressing for home, so the "modern look" dissolved the differentiation between a railroad carriage, a lunch counter, a night club lobby, a domestic window seat, a breakfast nook, and a dressing table. By the end of the Great Depression, the entire plot of a film such as *Mildred Pierce* could hinge on a child's quest to leave the now shameful, dark, upholstered romance of a Mediterranean house in pursuit of the well-lit glamour – steel windows, "airplane seats," and sweeping stairs – of a house to glide around in, backlit by sunshine.

Clothing manufacturers followed suit. Their first "California casuals" introduced new styles that followed the changing aesthetics of the home, drawing successively on Progressive Era dress reform, the busy gingham checks and flannels of the American cowgirl, and adaptations of pertinent exoticisms such as Andalusian gypsy dress. Models posed loosely but in repose. Within ten years, the emphasis, first borrowed from Elsa Schiaparelli and then re-exported back to her, was on a single line, a soft fabric, a solid colour, all of which exaggerated the expression of motion. Models now showed off a golf swing, slid into an open car, climbed an airport ramp, or swept down a staircase. The sense of mobile, twenty-four-hour glamour which these new design ideas carried seemed right for a city that, until late in the Second World War, had fewer children and more young unmarried adults than any other metropolis in the world. By 1939, the casual clothes of its now burgeoning textile industry – already recognizable enough to be famously satirized in *The Women* – were firmly attached to adult notions of sex and seduction.

Southern California, as the centre of the Allies' aircraft industry and the leading transfer point for shipping troops, munitions, and supplies to the Pacific, experienced a wartime boom that led to a tidal wave of growth – not only in housing and population but in the supply services, the distributive infrastructure, and the textiles, clothing, and other light industries that supported its military role. Los Angeles thus unconsciously equipped itself for the massive immigration that followed. Two days' leave in Hollywood was enough to persuade a million young soldiers and sailors to start their new lives in the sun; three years of tropical service had already taught them how to dress for it – from khaki shorts and chinos to the shirts they discovered in Hawaii. Scarcity, mass production, and military priorities combined to show Los Angeles industry how to produce clothing that was skimpier and cheaper, houses that could be built faster and more efficiently, and domestic equipment that could mimic the military in economy and utility, all making it easier for mothers to work outside the home.

The result was a lifestyle centred on a minimum, hygienic, one-storey house that could be bought on a veteran's loan, expand as the family grew, and use its garden to extend private living, entertaining, and work space; a home that could open itself up to allow the children to play, a father to read, a neighbour to drop by, and a mother to cook – all within earshot and eyeshot of each other. In came carports, barbecues, patios, sliding doors, strollers, open plans, and labour-saving appliances. Out went locked doors, staircases, gates, walls, steps, or anything else that might obstruct movement among them. This was the domestic ideal relentlessly marketed and adopted overseas, along with the American cars and appliances that made it work. In the permeable and visible surroundings that it produced – where children were constantly in sight, where patios served as entertainment centres, where floors and garden benches served as furniture and barbecues as ovens – presentable casual clothing stopped being a choice and became an imperative. By 1949, sportswear manufacturers in Los Angeles had joined this international bandwagon and gained a share of the global clothing market, second only to that of New York.

In styling this wear, there were repeated efforts, especially in films, to retain and then recapture the glamour and sophistication of the casual tradition of the 1930s. But it is hard to imagine that extravagant sportswear such as Lana Turner's white two-piece summer suit in *The Postman Always Rings Twice* or Jane Russell's shipboard deck ensemble in *Gentlemen Prefer Blondes* would suit the average postwar

Julius Shulman, Drake Residence, 1946, © J. Paul Getty Trust.
Used with permission, Julius Shulman Photography Archive
Research Library at the Getty Research Institute

housewife. More practical would be Hahn Cole's sunwear, shown in a cross-promotion with Ford Motors. Cole's models showed no less skin, but to make the glamorous attainable, the design was seamless, allowing no one element – the models, the clothes, or the car – to overshadow the other.

By the time Bonnie Cashin fled to New York to adapt what remained of the adult tradition in California clothing to high fashion, the sources for loungewear were no longer Paris or the luxury liner but the everyday bathing suit, the car hop's uniform, the poolside, the patio, and especially the kindergarten and playground. For the postwar boom had transformed Raymond Chandler's hard-boiled city of the 1930s, a place in love with youthfulness but without much youth, into Gidgetville, home to the Brady Bunch and the Partridges. It had become a wide-eyed city of hope and wonder whose cultural landscape, from home to highway, was made for kids. Only five years (1950–55) mark the gulf that Nicholas Ray traverses as he moves from *In a Lonely Place*, where desperately courageous adult solitudes conspire in black and grey closed courtyards, to the technicoloured vistas of *Rebel without a Cause*. Here, in a vast sunlit suburb, confident children of the freeways make an open society out of doors. Indoors, their timid and helpless small town parents cower amid the wilderness of a panoramic city.

Climate was obviously a critical factor in making practicable this horizontal, mobile, wide-screen flow of visible movement between places and events, indoors and out. But as advertising media moved, one by one, into colour, the sun and blue sky became integral to the creation of the vivid legends through which new loans for new architecture, new cars, and new furnishings could all be promoted together. Looking back at the ads in magazines from 1955 to 1965, it becomes almost impossible to know which of the products is being sold. Is it the model, the sportswear, the automobile, the house, the furnishings, or simply the summer weather and its pursuits? It is equally difficult to distinguish the golden murals on the street façades of the city's leading home savings banks (none of which picture a home, but all of which display sun, seagulls, bathing suits, orange trees, and children) from the collages in a tourist or hotel brochure. Those murals are fitting predictions of the panoramic spirit of the open plan, freeway, drive-in culture of Angelenos in the late 1950s and the 1960s, where home, garden, highway, beach, and playground have merged.

Much of this sense of an open society was in fact made real. By 1960, the city was becoming fully equipped to service its children. Sparkling new public schools, recreation centres, and branch libraries were rising as fast as the lifeguard stations on the beaches. They were also rising as fast as the thousands of coffee shops, drive-ins, and fast food stands through which kids could have access – whether in front of the counter or behind – to a democratic version of café society. And to everyone leaving a California high school, a four-year college education was opened. By August 1965, when those left out of this dream began to burn it down, the ideal of life in southern California had become a sort of holiday on wheels – a society of possibility, convenience, and pleasure. It had turned into a society in which cooking, cleaning, commuting, study, and work had become, in every sense, "child's play."

This seems to be the right term, for as the Sixties neared, a wonderful sense of ease and confidence seemed to take hold of design. What careless spirit was abroad to name a hamburger stand after the atom or the bikini after an island it destroyed? Architects now began to play with the precedents established for economy and efficiency in postwar living space and to adapt the scale and terms of the domestic aesthetic to places of work, service, and ceremony. John Lautner set one early example by designing a home whose walls, with their built-in furniture, rolled out to unfold the entire house, like petals opening to the sun. Raphael Soriano reduced the house to nothing but a penetrable steel pavilion that provided occasional enclosure from which to enjoy the outdoor courts and terraces. Then, in the same way, he designed various horizontal glass buildings where every work space opened onto a garden and every staff cafeteria sat in a court, all as casually as the new house fitted itself around its kitchen and its patio.

From the first, casual clothes had gone with casual posture and with constant movement, as mannequins with buttocks on the floor or hands on the hip made clear. Borrowing from designs for outdoor furnishings, the height, economy, and line of indoor furniture now responded: counters to lean on, benches to talk on, the same benches to lie on, stools to swivel on, and slung-back chairs to go with sling-back clothes. All were neutral in their approach to posture and deportment, could be sat on or moved off without adjustment to dress, and designed to work equally well whether one was alone or in company. Hence, the visible differences between public and private space, school and home, coffee shop and church disappeared. In consequence, and

Julius Shulman, William S. Beckett, Cooper Residence, 1960, © J. Paul Getty Trust. Used with permission, Julius Shulman Photography Archive Research Library at the Getty Research Institute

as the neutrality of the glass-walled interior increased, the visual organization of space began to depend on accents, especially accents with colour, and especially when used for publicity. Fabrics and furnishing, including what one wore, now worked with everything else in California – its rebounding sentimentality about fruit farming, the hoopla that came with admitting Hawaii to the union, and the crude beginnings of colour television – to give primacy not only to the "living colours" of the primary palette but also to the free movements and simple shapes that went along with it in every modernist's idea of how to create an ideal childhood.

So the body and the incidentals now dressed the architecture, and cross-promoting them became a daily habit as much as a publicity

Julius Shulman, Buff Straub Hensman, Mirman Residence, 1960 (detail), © J. Paul Getty Trust. Used with permission, Julius Shulman Photography Archive Research Library at the Getty Research Institute

stunt. As an editorial in *Vogue* suggested, California now showed it was possible once again to "dress well and stay at home." The proud new owners of a home by Buff Straub Hensman showed off it – and their athletic good looks – perfectly by coordinating their casuals with the fabric on the benches and the fruit on the kitchen counter. It was also possible *not* to dress well and go out. A study for the civic centre of a proposed new city on the Ahmanson Ranch, done about 1965, shows nothing but a symphony of trellises and terrace chairs, in which all animation and conspicuous incident come from the coloured shirts and slacks of those who will move around it. In such an environment, dressing down and moving around got you noticed, and this, after all, was a city of display.

Both the lounging posture and the refusal to distinguish between place and occasion met some initial resistance, especially abroad. How many Sixties teenagers doing nothing must have been tormented by the command to sit up straight? And imagine the bafflement of Mitzi Gaynor, in London in 1958 for the opening of *South Pacific*, when she was forced to check out of the Dorchester for walking into the dining room for breakfast in the very shorts the film was celebrating. But by the time the last late-night television shows have moved to Burbank, an entire world of "slacks" and "loafers" is in place: Johnny Carson is ready to lose his ties; Judy Garland's capri pants and casual tops have won the day for showtime; and boys and girls of all ages are busy shopping in Carnaby Street or the Via della Spiga.

Meanwhile, in Los Angeles, the great studios collapse; its moguls go mad; Boeing moves to Seattle; there are earthquakes, freeway pile-ups, fires, riots, deaths, and smog; the very television presenters who donned the city's styles make them the butt of a national joke.

Angelenos start both to hanker for the gritty city that, along with Bunker Hill, seemed to disappear in the last stage of suburbanization, or gleefully to register, along with Ed Ruscha and John Boorman, its most extravagant corners of banality. With its once wild growth in clear contraction and its everyday life poised to recapture the hints of foreboding and disaster that had so long animated its literature, the city could wake up, perhaps, some sunny morning in 1967, to recognize that its erstwhile optimism had taken over the world and that it was now responsible for a worldwide vision of youthful living, advanced by the same interests – aircraft, movies, automobiles, and appliances – which the whole country was exporting, alongside the films and television shows that portrayed them. Yet the city that made these dreams was barely producing them anymore.

One designer, in particular, catches this changing spirit. In 1953 we find Rudi Gernreich selling four postwar dreams together, portraying Lauren Bacall against her Craig Ellwood house, in capri slacks and a little flared shift, and with an obvious perky readiness either to reach for the floor and pick up her baby or to jump when someone whistles. At the height of LA confidence, Gernreich dreams up the topless dress to go with the doorless house. But by early 1965, he takes his casuals out with James Coburn – an international symbol of the violence now inherent in California's modernity – to the Watts Towers. This scrappy piece of folk art lay in the neighbourhood that had been left out of the casual dream, isolated to its poor, and remembered forever six months later when it exploded in rebellion. Here he draped his mannequins around the monument and suffused them in premonitory sunset pink.

A little earlier, Gernreich had taken a new men's line to the city's open schoolyards, now police-fenced and gang-trashed, where his models slouched and sprawled along the decaying remnants of sites once managed as the ideal of hygienic childhood. Finally, tongue in cheek, he sets his models against nothing but light, making high casual fashion from the boot, the ski mask, and the machine gun of the urban revolutionary. There, the slouch has gone, the accoutrements of the city are missing, and the single-minded models are poised and ready for revolt. Is it cynicism, romanticism, or simply modish irony that thus filters urban decay and commercializes social resistance into something as apparently trivial as style? Or perhaps a better question, is style trivial after all, or is that where the subtler substance shows?

SOURCES AND READINGS

This essay draws on research for a study of the relationship between architecture and culture in Los Angeles from 1920 to 1970, originating with and funded by the French Ministry of Culture, the National Building Museum (Washington, DC), and the Centre Canadien d'Architecture (Montreal, Que) in preparation for a planned exhibition.

It is grounded first on an intensive reading of the astonishingly thoroughgoing original record of work by architects in Los Angeles, documenting the sophisticated design process behind every emerging typology, from coffee shops and drive-in markets to the transparent home. Note especially the heroically extensive architectural archives at University of California Santa Barbara, as well as other essential collections of archives at UCLA, California Polytechnic University Pomona, the Huntington Library, the Getty Research Institute, and the California State Library in Sacramento. Other sources are the papers of Raymond Kappe, Pierre Koenig, and John Lautner at the Getty Research Institute, Los Angeles; of Robert Alexander at Cornell University; of Charles and Ray Eames at the Prints and Photographs Division of the Library of Congress; of Eckbo, Royston and Williams at the School of Environmental Design of the University of California, Berkeley; of Cram, Goodhue and Ferguson at the Avery Library of Columbia University; and of Harwell Hamilton Harris at the Alexander Library, University of Texas,

Austin; also used – most generously on their part – were the office archives of Armet and Davis, Canadian masters of the drive-in, in Los Angeles. The archives of Olmsted and Olmsted at the Olmsted Historic Site in Brookline, Massachussets, are essential for the planning histories of key subdivisions. A rich body of aerial and street photographs of Los Angeles in development is housed in the Huntington Library and the University of Southern California and at the Library of Congress and the Los Angeles Public Library, where much is available online.

The published literature related to this history is vast and growing. Studies of central figures and movements in the architectural history of Los Angeles – Richard Neutra, Rudolf Schindler, Frank Lloyd Wright, and the Case Study House program – are already long-established. The pioneering writings of Esther McCoy and David Gebhard, along with reprinted compendia of selections from the magazine [California] *Arts and Architecture* and the many published representations of the architectural photography of Julius Shulman, were until recently the key secondary sources on architects of the postwar generation. But in the last ten years a flurry of full-length monographs – on architects John Lautner, Harwell Harris, Craig Ellwood, Rafael Soriano, and A. Quincy Jones, among others – has begun to be available.

For data on the patterns of growth and mobility in southern California, I would draw particular attention to Scott Bottles, *Los Angeles and the Automobile: The Making of the Modern City* (1991) and Richard Longstreth, *The Drive-In, the Supermarket, and the Transformation of Commercial Space in Los Angeles, 1914–41* (1998); on homes and housing, Merry Ovnick, *Los Angeles: The End of the Rainbow* (1994); on planning, Greg Hise and William Deverell, *Magnetic Los Angeles: Planning the Twentieth Century Metropolis* (1997); and on the impact of economic and demographic shifts, the studies of Kevin Starr, especially his *Embattled Dreams: California in War and Peace, 1940–50*.

There is an abundance, perhaps a surplus, of reflective essays on the nature, mythologies, and social geography of Los Angeles, of which Reyner Banham's paean, *Los Angeles: The Architecture of Four Ecologies* (1973), and Mike Davis's dyspeptic responses to it, *City of Quartz* (1990) and *Ecology of Fear* (1998), have been the most influential. I would turn first, though, to works of a quieter temper, such as William Alexander McClung's alliance of social geography to literature in *Landscapes of Desire: Anglo Mythologies of Los Angeles* (2002) and Edward Soja's imaginative geohistorical reading of the city as *Thirdspace: Journeys to Los Angeles and Other Real-and-Imagined Places* (1996). Most especially, however, the enormous literary and artistic observatory that has charted a uniquely changeable narrative history for Los

Angeles – in words and images – provides the real introduction to its psyche and to the dispersal of its mores. This can be found among sources as varied as the contemporaneous journalism of such figures as Edmund Wilson (observing the "Great Bubble" of the 1920s), Carey McWilliams (whose *Southern California: An Island on the Land* holds near-biblical status in this arena), Blaise Cendrars (on Hollywood just before the war), and the early Tom Wolfe; the photographic odysseys of the postwar era published by artists from Robert Frank to Ed Ruscha; memoirs – some masquerading as novels – like those of M.F.K. Fisher on the Teens, John Fante on the Depression era, or Nora Ephron, Susan Sontag, D.J. Waldie, James Ellroy, and Leslie Epstein on postwar suburban life; satires such as Upton Sinclair's *Oil!* in the 1920s, Aldous Huxley's *After Many a Summer Dies the Swan*, Nathanael West's *Day of the Locust*, and F. Scott Fitzgerald's *The Last Tycoon* for the 1930s, and Evelyn Waugh's *The Loved One* for the 1950s, and thrillers like those of Raymond Chandler, James M. Cain, Mickey Spillane, and (most acutely on the "casual") Ross MacDonald.

For three fiction films that best captured the "casual" context of their different moments, I might propose *What Price Hollywood?* (Cukor 1932); *The Best Years of Our Lives* (Wyler 1946); and, though it is often visually pedestrian, Mike Nichols's *The Graduate* (filmed in 1965 but issued in 1967). Most pertinent to the concluding statements in this essay is John Boorman's dystopic *Point Blank* (1967), and in my final nod towards the wry self-conscious Los Angeles of the last generation, I am thinking of the forty years of lovingly lurid nostalgias that start with the rather terrible *Harlow* (1965) but take flight after Polanski's *Chinatown* (1974). A fine reading of the tradition with a superb compilation of clips is Thom Andersen's *Los Angeles Plays Itself* (2004), while Edward Dimendberg's recent *Film Noir and the Spaces of Modernity* helps relate one distinctive film genre to the modern spaces addressed in this essay. It is important to acknowledge, however, that from the 1950s onwards, California style and the desire for California living was exported as much through such vehicles as *Dragnet*, *Adam-12*, family comedies, and the *Burns and Allen Show*, or in film series such as *Gidget* and the Beach Blanket sagas, as through classic film dramas.

Thanks to Denise Bratton, who contributed significantly to research for this essay.

Contributors

Dimitry Anastakis, Department of History, Trent University

Gretta Chambers, chancellor emerita, McGill University

Olivier Courteaux, Department of History, Ryerson University

Christopher Dummitt, Department of History, Trent University

Frances Early, Department of History, Mount Saint Vincent University

Kristy Holmes, Department of Fine Arts, Mount Allison University

Marcel Martel, Department of History, York University

Nicholas Olsberg, Canadian Centre for Architecture

France Vanlaethem, Département de design, Université du Québec à Montréal

Krys Verrall, Division of Humanities and Fine Arts Cultural Studies, York University

modernist movement in, 12; and modernity, 128, 130, 133–4, 140; preservation of buildings and the past, 134–6, 138; rural, 135; Sixties as a unique period for the history of, 129–32; social responsibility, 131–2; urban neighbourhoods, 140

Architecture, bâtiment, construction, 129

Architecture Canada, 129. *See also* *Journal of the Royal Architectural Institute of Canada*

Armatage, Kay, 62

art, 10, 12, 154; visual, 10; and relationship to space and social movement, 154

artists, 5, 56–7; Joyce Wieland as an, 56–7

automobile, 10–11, 71–92, 170–1, 172, 174, 179; accidents, 72, 73, 74, 76–7, 78, 81, 86; and advertising, 75, 170–1, 174; animal metaphor, 78; and architecture, 135; breadwinner ideology, 72–3, 82, 91; and codes of behaviour, 72; education, 81–2; enforcement of rules and regulatory mechanisms, 82–6, 88; engineering, 79–81; experts, 76–80, 86; highway system, 12; idealism, 10–11; and juvenile delinquency, 85–6; and modernism, 74, 86; and modern urban planning and renewal, 89–90; ownership, 74; postwar manhood, 83–5, 87, 91; and press, 76–7, 78, 84; and reasonable man ideology, 73; and safety advocates, 77; and women, 75, 170–1. *See also* drunk driving

avant-garde, 146, 147–51, 162

baby boomers, 4
Baraka, Amiri, 145, 147, 148, 162
Beatles, 4, 19
Beatniks, 11
beautification, 152–3, 160–1; as centennial project, 153
Beckett, William S., 177
Bégin, Monique, 52
biculturalism, 8, 25, 54
bilingualism, 25, 61–2
black cultural activism, 145
Bloc, André, 137–8
Blouin, André, 127, 137
Blumenfeld, Hans, 140
Born at the Right Time (Owram), 6
Boston, Helen, 37
Boudreau, André, 101
Bougie, Marcel, 105
Bourassa, Robert, 103
British Columbia Automobile Association (BCAA), 75, 81
British Columbia Medical Association, 84
British Columbia Ministry of Highways, 75
British Columbia Safety Council, 79
Bryce, W.A., 71–2
bureaucrats, 100, 101–2, 108, 111–12; historiography of, 108; and influence on planning and implementing government policies, 100; and OPTAT, 101–2, 108

Caisse de dépôt et placement, 23
California, 171, 172–3, 176, 177

Combined Universities Campaign for Nuclear Disarmament (CUCND), 7

Commission of Inquiry into the Non-Medical Use of Drugs (Le Dain Commission), 101

Commission of Inquiry on Health and Social Welfare (Castonguay-Nepveu Commission), 103

Committee on Equality for Women (CEW), 52

conceptual art, 148

conflict, 5

conservatism, 18–19

constitutional and jurisdictional conflict, 108–9

constitutional reform, 47

construction of Canada as female, 61

consumer, 12

consumerism, 5

consumption, 74

Council on Drug Abuse (CODA), 110, 111

counterculture, 9, 99, 105

Creighton, Thomas H., 137

culture, 5; architectural culture, 12

Dainton, D.G., 85

Death and Life of Great American Cities, The (Jacobs), 89–90, 135

de Gaulle, Charles, 11, 116–25; and Canadian alliances, 119–20; concept of history, 120–1; concept of independence, 122, 124; and development of French-Canadian relations, 116, 117–20; legacy in Quebec, 124–5; and Quebec sovereignty, 118; significance of state visits, 118; state visit to Canada (1944), 116, 118; (1945), 116, 119; (1967), 121; and support for Quebec independence, 121–5; "Vive le Québec libre!", 117

Democratic Convention in Chicago, 6

Desbarats, Guy, 139

Deschamps, Yvon, 20

de Sève, Micheline, 54

Diamond, A.J., 153–4

Diefenbaker, John, 6

Drexler, Arthur, 158, 159, 161

drugs, 11, 99–112; and bureaucracy, 101–12; and educational strategies, 99, 101, 103, 105–7, 108, 111; and experts, 106–7; federal law on, 103; legalization and decriminalization of, 99, 111; and medicalization, 107, 108, 112; as medical problem, 99–100; as moral weakness, 99; prevention, 103; as public health problem, 99; as socially acceptable, 99; as social practice, 105–6; treatment of and rehabilitation, 99, 103

drunk driving, 83–5; Breathalyzer, 83–4; and drinking as symbol of civilized behaviour, 84

Duckworth, Muriel, 36

Duplessis, Maurice, 4, 130

economy, 21–3; in Quebec, 21–3

education, 18, 19. *See also* students

Ellwood, Craig, 179

engineering, 79–81

equality, 51–6. *See also* women

experts, 73, 75, 76–86, 151; and links to modernity and masculinity, 73;

modernist architectural movement, 12

modernity, 22, 47–8, 54, 71, 72, 74–9, 81, 83–6, 92, 128, 130, 140; and architecture, 128, 130, 140; car accidents as failure in, 86; and escapism, 75–6; and experts, 86; and masculinity, 73–6, 92; and postwar manhood, 83–5; in Quebec, 130; and technology, 71, 75, 79, 81

modernization, 128; social in Quebec, 130

Montreal, 4, 12, 20, 117, 121, 127, 128, 133, 135; modernization of, 128, 138

Montreal police strike, 167

Morris, Cerise, 53

Mouffe, 20

multiculturalism, 48–9, 54

multiracial society, 5

Museum of Modern Art (MoMA), 146, 156, 158

music, 19–20

Nader, Ralph, 73–4, 78, 81, 86–8, 90, 91

Narcotic Control Act, 110

National Action Committee on the Status of Women (NAC), 53

"national consensus," 49–51

National Gallery of Canada, 62, 64

National Housing Act, 133, 138

National Liberation Front of South Vietnam, 36

National Liberation Front Red Cross for Children, 34

nationalism, 7, 11, 46, 49–51, 54, 65; liberal civic, 65. *See also* Canadian nationalism; Quebec nationalism

national unity, 45, 47, 50, 52, 54, 61, 63, 64–5; and feminism, 52; Trudeau's concept of, 45–7, 50, 61, 64–5

Nelson, Jennifer, 161

New Brunswick, 7

"New City, The," 146, 154, 156, 158, 160, 161, 162

New Democratic Party, 7

New Left, 7

"new nationalism," 7

"New Treason of the Intellectuals," 48–9

New York, 12, 56–7, 58, 77, 146, 147, 151, 152, 156, 158, 162; Joyce Wieland in, 56–7; World's Fair, 167–8

Non-Partisan Association (NPA), 89

Nova Scotia College of Art and Design (NSCAD), 146, 147–9, 161–2; as part of redevelopment, 161–2; transformation of during 1960s, 147–8

Nova Scotia Project (NSP), 148–9, 160–2

nuclear war, 25

nuclear weapons policy, 37

O Canada, 63–4

O'Connell, Sean, 77

October Crisis, 9, 21

Office de la prévention et du traitement de l'alcoolisme et des autres toxicomanies (OPTAT), 100–12; comparison with ARF, 103–5, 111–12; creation of, 101–2; education,

105–6; funding, 102; influence on public debate, 107; medical experts of, 108; Ministry of Social Affairs, 108; and Quebec bureaucracy, 101–2; research, 104; and state, 101–3

Official Traffic Commission, (OTC), 78, 80

Old Dolls for Peace, 34

Ontario government, 11

Ontario VOW Knitting Project for Vietnamese Children, 31–2. *See also* Voice of Women of Canada

Orangeburg Massacre, 168

Organization Man, 87, 88, 91

Ottawa, 128

Our Lives: Canada after 1945 (Finkel), 6

Owram, Doug, 6

Pal, Leslie, 52, 53–4

Parkins, Wendy, 30, 37

Partial Nuclear Test Ban Treaty (1963), 25

Pateman, Carole, 55–6, 61

peace movement, 26, 27, 28, 33, 36, 37; international women's, 28, 33, 36; U.S. women's, 37

Pearson, Lester, 26, 27, 52, 117, 152

Phillips, Anne, 55, 61

Place Ville Marie, 20, 127, 128, 132, 138

Postman Always Rings Twice, The, 173

postmodern, 11–12; style, 11–12, 152

posture, 176–7, 178–9

poverty, 150, 155, 158, 162; and perceived social ills, 159–60

press, 21–3; and automobile, 78, 84; CBC, 21; and car accidents, 76–7; "The Province in Print," 21

Progressive Architecture, 137

production, 74

protest, 6–7, 8, 9, 10, 29, 30; humanitarian knitting projects, 9; maternalist approach to, 9, 30; quilt, 10; social, 26; and Vietnam, 8

"Province in Print, The," 21

public art, 12

public housing developments, 146, 155–6

public memory, 3

Quebec, 4, 7, 9, 18, 19–20, 21–3, 127, 130; citizens, 20; civil rights movement in, 7; economy, 21–3; entertainment, 19–20; government, 11, 102–3, 107–8, 116–17; historical memory, 22; Historical Monuments Act, 135; Liberals, 4, 22, 122–3; music, 19–20; political changes during 1960s, 116–17; politics, 18, 23; press, 21–2; provincial-federal relations, 116–17; reforms, 130; social change, 19–21, 23; students, 9. *See also* Quiet Revolution

Quebec City, 135

"Quebec model," 7, 21–2

Quebec nationalism, 11, 46, 49, 54, 121–5; and de Gaulle's support for, 121–5

Québécois, 4, 7, 19, 20, 47

Quebec state, 102–3, 108–9

Quiet Revolution, 5, 7, 9, 22–3, 122, 130–1